W0309016

The Master's Plan
Copyright © 2022
All rights reserved.

First Edition
English

ISBN: 9798839326866

Gutenbergst. 12, 65321 Heidenrod, Germany
triamba@gmail.com

A heartfelt Gratitude to Gurudev,
the Soul of this book and the
Sunshine of our lives.

My Thanks to Gauri, Rachel, Savitri Dasi,
Sonja and Vrajmohan Das for their support.

# THE MASTER'S PLAN

My Life Experiences
*with*
Paramahamsa Vishwananda

# Table of Contents

# The Beginning

It was in 2002 when someone told me that a great Master had reincarnated. He was described as a playful young man from Mauritius who often visited Europe.

At that time, I was still living in Austria. I had just quit my job and was about to leave for India to go to the *ashram* of Sri Sathya Sai Baba. Around the same time, I had read the book, *The Autobiography of a Yogi* and developed a strong pull towards Mahavatar Babaji, a timeless yogi from the Himalayas.

For various reasons, I convinced myself that it was not the time to pursue a meeting with the young Mauritian Master and proceeded with the preparations for my upcoming journey to the *ashram*.

Upon arriving in India, I was surprised that a few people at the *ashram* also knew about this 'young saint' with the name *Visham*.

There was a woman from Switzerland with whom I spent a lot of time and who was especially captivated by Visham's miracles, materialisations, and wisdom. She mentioned He had predicted that His official mission was going to start soon and spread worldwide. On one occasion, she even stressed, 'His teaching will be spread much in the Eastern European Countries. You are from there. Maybe you will be with Him?' Her words were inviting and vibrant. As a result, I found myself pulled to meet this saint upon my return to Europe.

While still at the *ashram*, my roommate there showed me a photo of a young, beautiful Indian man in a red t-shirt, with long black hair, looking up slightly, seemingly engrossed in something. The picture resonated strongly with me, but when I enquired about Him, my roommate couldn't remember His name. Later I found out that this captivating individual was, indeed, Visham.

My entire time in India was long and intense. This was my third visit to the *ashram* of Sathya Sai Baba, as I had great respect for him as a *guru*. He had initiated my spiritual path beautifully and showed me the way out of this mundane, materialistic life – a life which was no longer satisfactory for me. Despite living in Germany and having a good job and a husband, I felt deeply unfulfilled. Something essential was missing, but at that time, I didn't know what it was.

I grew up in a Communist country and in an atheistic family. I didn't have any understanding of who God could be or even who Christ was. As a child, I remember asking my parents about the vastness of the universe and about death, but I never received an answer apart from, 'Don't bother yourself with such things'. I loved my country (at that time Yugoslavia) and I experienced a lot of freedom as a child. I had good friends and was surrounded by family.

After my father received a better position as a teacher abroad, we moved from Yugoslavia to Germany. I was excited about the new country and the language, but it took me years to adapt to, and accept, the gloomy weather and the different mentality of the people.

I was not educated much on human values by my family. My father had occasional personality problems and, at times, abused alcohol. My mother was oppressed by him but was always there for us children with a calm spirit and the ability to endure the most difficult situations. Due to their difficult marriage, my childhood innocence didn't last long and I was forced to grow up fast and stand on my own two feet.

Accordingly, my youth was not straightforward. I didn't know what to do in life or which direction to go in. I drifted from one experience to the other, which painfully shaped my character and paved the direction of my life path throughout the years. With the passing of time, I started becoming more aware of my behaviours, emotions, and the need for inner balance.

When I was nineteen, I met my future husband and two years later we were married in

Germany. Whatever was still missing materially in my life started to manifest during these years. Eventually, we both had good jobs and all the means for having a family. Yet something inside of me was not ready for that step. A feeling of senselessness started to dominate my life and, despite trying to divert my attention and busy myself with other things, these feelings came up again and again. I started searching for alternative, therapeutic support and came across the practice of meditation. It was around this time that, after five years of marriage, I separated from my husband to live alone for a period of time.

I soon learned about Sai Baba and his *ashram* in India from researching online. My English teacher, who happened to know some people from the Sathya Sai Organisation in Germany, arranged a meeting with them. The gathering was in a small house outside the city, where regular lectures and spiritual singing (*bhajans*) took place. My intention was to just get some information about the *ashram* in India and leave but, as they invited me to stay, I joined their gathering.

It was very strange to hear the *bhajans* in Sanskrit, 'Rama, Krishna, Govinda…', and I wished to leave but, since the room was cramped and overcrowded, many people would have needed to stand up because of me, so I stayed. To my astonishment, after the gathering, I felt such peace and relief in my whole being and I took it as a sign to follow this path.

Someone from the Sai Centre gave me a few books for reading which revived within me an understanding for my need of spirituality. The perception that we are embodied souls and not just a body, and the possibility that God could exist, started to awaken in my heart. Through these books, I learned about the ancient Vedic laws of *karma* and reincarnation, and how they naturally explain the reasons for various human destinies. Life does not just happen by coincidence but is rather a continuation of previous lives, with a greater purpose and plan than we are usually aware of. This helped me to realise the reason for my aversion towards eating meat and I became vegetarian overnight.

Each of my three visits to the Sai Baba's *ashram* in India brought about big personal transformations, opening me to new horizons and opportunities, and bringing new people into my life. I was thirsty to explore more; to know about *yoga*, Hinduism and Christianity, the reasons for diversity of religions, and for our forgetfulness.

After my first visit to India, I left Germany and moved to Austria, where I was alone. My intention was to dive deeper into spiritual study and to detach more from my family and my ex-husband.

I received a good job in a pharmaceutical company and a cosy apartment in Vienna, where I could rollerblade to my office and enjoy the beautiful places in the city and its surroundings.

I didn't befriend many people and used my free time for reading, studying and attending spiritual gatherings. My interests had completely changed, which naturally distanced me from my old friends and invited some new people into my life.

Over the two years I spent in Austria, I acquired a lot of spiritual understanding. Still, there was something crying deep inside of me. My mind was active, curious and uncontrolled and I didn't know what to do.

I considered changing my job and starting some humanitarian work but I couldn't see the ways or means of achieving this objective. The problem was obviously inside of me, and I finally decided to leave Austria and travel again to the Sai Baba's *ashram* to work more on myself.

While in India, Sai Baba never talked to me personally. I had many meaningful dreams and felt his inner guidance, but I would still occasionally wish for a guide with whom I could personally interact. When I saw him the last time, he made a sign to me indicating that I needed to be patient.

After India, I returned to Serbia with the intention of offering *hatha-yoga* classes and inspiring people with spirituality. I had become a *yoga* instructor over time and was eager to share it with others.

It felt good to be back in my homeland. I was able to spend some time with my sister and her three little daughters, my grandpa, and the rest of my family. Staying in my parent's house with my grandpa, I was able to dedicate a lot of creative time to painting and designing our living space.

The *yoga* classes were running well and I met several people who were interested in spirituality. In Serbia, however, *yoga* was not highly accepted at that time and some people from my town began to publicly accuse me of sectarianism. Consequently, after one year, I decided to leave Serbia and moved back to Austria.

It was only once I was living in Austria again that I eventually tried to search for Visham, who was now called Sri Swami Vishwananda.

# The Meeting

When I first came back to Austria, I stayed in a house of Sai Baba devotees near Vienna and began searching for an adequate job. With time, I found a job and also began a three-year long study on Social Pedagogics in Vienna.

Over the years, several unusual sensations started to develop within me. I could feel something inside my body which wasn't physical but was still very tangible. It would move and then dissolve with an accelerated pressure coming up from my abdominal area and was often followed by a strong burning sensation. At other times, I could hear an inner voice, usually explaining or predicting something to me.

I was also having many dreams. From childhood, my dreams were vivid but after beginning my spiritual journey, they started transforming into spontaneous visions which I could often not put into words.

For example, one day during a nap, I perceived myself in a room and heard a knock on the door. I opened it and saw a nun, dressed fully in black, looking deeply into my eyes. I shut the door in front of her, wondering to myself what a nun would want from me.

These experiences were generally overwhelming. So much so, that they created a great amount of tension and confusion within my mind.

After separating from my husband, there were a few attempts to re-establish our relationship over the years but we hit a dead end each time.

Our paths were going in different directions: he still wanted to enjoy worldly pleasures while I was pulled more and more towards spirituality. The whole separation process was tedious, and it was only after visiting a renowned astrologer that I made the final decision to cut off the relationship with him even though we still shared an attachment to one another.

At this point in my life, I was now free enough to make up my mind to search for Swami Vishwananda. I came across some inspiring testimonials from His devotees on the internet and to my surprise, I also found a web page where I could request a personal interview with Him.

Several weeks passed and then a response came with an invitation for an appointment on November 2, 2004. As my divorced parents were both still living in Germany, I combined my trip to meet Swami Vishwananda with visiting them.

Upon arriving in Germany, I went to see my mother, with whom I had a very close relationship. I told her about my plans to go and meet Swami

Vishwananda and she decided to join me. Together, we drove by car to a private house in a small town where Swami was giving interviews.

I vividly remember my first sight of Him. He suddenly came out of His room dressed in the orange robes of an Indian *swami*. His appearance was so radiant and pure that I felt shy just looking at Him. When He called us inside His room, I tried to hide my shyness and gave Him a rose, saying 'Sai Ram', which is a common greeting among the Sai Baba devotees. He took the flower and responded with 'Jai Gurudev', which is a common greeting among His devotees.

The scent in His room was divine, and my eyes fell immediately upon a picture of Shirdi Sai Baba, which was covered with self-manifested *vibhuti* (sacred ash).

When we all sat down, He politely asked what He could do for us. I had prepared a whole list of questions and was about to start, but He looked at my mother first and waited for her to answer. My mother didn't know what to say since she was just accompanying me and eventually asked about her health. Swami gave her a holy oil to massage on the affected parts of her body and then materialised a pendant for her with Shirdi Sai Baba on it. To our surprise, He did it right in front of our eyes and with such humility, as if it was the most normal thing in the world. He then turned to me and waited for my questions.

Slightly anxious and in broken English, I expressed my concern about my life situation. I mentioned the relationship with my ex-husband and the attachment we still had to one another. Swami listened to me, though I felt that it was not only my words He was hearing but that He was listening to and perceiving what was inside of me. With a calm voice he said:

'This, that is between you two, is love.'

I first wondered about this since I thought that we were just attached to each other. So, I asked him, slightly confused, 'Is he my husband?'

'He is your *karmic* husband,' Swami answered.

'Is it good to let go of him?', I inquired.

'Yes,' He replied softly, 'Is this difficult for you?'

He asked this, with such mercy and brilliance in His eyes, that I knew it wouldn't be difficult anymore. His words instantly transformed my limited view of our relationship into a wider, selfless perspective and I could naturally let go.

He asked me to relay a message to my ex-husband to work on himself and predicted an imminent change in my life.

'You have to trust more,' He emphasised, gesturing for me to come forward to receive His blessing.

I knelt down in front of Him. When He placed His right hand on my head, I felt electricity enter my body and run from my toes up towards my head. I had never experienced such intensity before. It was like recharging an empty battery.

At the time, I didn't know who Swami was or what my connection with Him might be, but I did recognise Him as someone very powerful and all-knowing, yet also accessible and who selflessly cares for others. At the end of the interview, I was so thankful that I asked if I could do something for Him.

'What would you do for me?' He smiled and asked me to leave my contact details.

After we left, my mother and I felt such intense love that the whole car was filled with it. We stopped a few times on the way home to look at His picture, which we bought during our visit, and again a stream of love would pour out of us. This was an incredibly uplifting experience; the first meeting with the *satguru*.

As Swami Vishwananda predicted, several changes happened shortly after. I found a new flat and received an additional job. Above all, He remained constantly on my mind. I talked about Him with everyone I could. While some people were inspired and wished to meet Him, others were quite sceptical.

In the time following my first meeting with Swami Vishwananda, my preoccupation was to calculate and plan when, where, and how I could meet Him again.

The next time I saw Swami was two months later in Munich for a Darshan, where hundreds of people had gathered to receive His blessing. My heart rejoiced when He entered the hall, wearing His silky robe with His long, dark hair falling loosely over His shoulders. He first gave a public talk and explained the importance and the role of the *guru*, which means the remover of ignorance. He said that the *guru* leads a disciple from the false outer identifications to the inner realisation of the blissful soul, which is a part of God.

To safely cross the mighty ocean of *samsara*, the cycle of birth and death, one needs a boatman, a *guru*, who knows the way. Without a *guru*, it is like a boat in the middle of the ocean, blown by the wind in different directions, never reaching its destination. I remember that everything He said was of great importance.

After the speech, Swami sang a *bhajan*, which sounded to me, deep inside my soul, like the voice of the shepherd calling his sheep to return. After He finished the *bhajan*, the singing was then taken over by the music band and the Darshan began.

People started lining up and approaching Him one by one for His blessing. Swami would place His thumb on the forehead (the third eye) while looking deeply into the eyes of each person. He revealed that He would actually look at the soul of every individual and remove the *karmic* obstacles from our path. When it was my turn, my heart was beating in my throat and again, a soothing electricity flowed throughout my whole body, flooding my mind with peace.

After the Darshan, we had the opportunity to personally meet Swami to ask a question but, at some point, the queue became so long that He discontinued taking questions. As it happened, He called out to the person standing right beside me, 'See you later, for dinner.' When I heard this, I so wished to be closer to Him and wistfully left the venue.

A few weeks later I travelled with a friend to the Shivaratri festival at the newly opened *ashram* and met Swami again. The *ashram* was located in Steffenshof, Germany, a small village with a few houses in the middle of the countryside. One of the three houses that comprised the *ashram* was the temple which had a small shop and a dining area.

Around a hundred people had gathered in the temple for this celebration. During the night, *abhishekam* and *puja* (devotional worship and prayers), were performed to Shiva. And while singing *bhajans*, we could observe Swami manifesting (giving birth to) *Shiva-lingams*, which are the symbol of Shiva in an egg-like form, out of His throat. The energy was elevating and everyone there felt immensely blessed.

During this event, Swami personally greeted me and asked about my mother. It surprised me that, despite so many people being around him, He still remembered me. In a childish way I wondered aloud, 'You remember me?' He replied in a similarly wondering tone, 'Of course I remember you', and then walked away… Every word He said was profoundly meaningful to me and I deeply cherished them.

It wasn't until Easter celebrations and a *yagna* (fire ceremony) in Italy, when I would see him again. I went with my mother and the same friend who came with me for Shivaratri. On Good Friday, Swami gave a valuable talk about the meaning of Easter. In His discourse, He brought about a deeper insight and understanding of Christ's life and teachings than I had ever heard before. Through it, Christ appeared so close and available; something which I had missed throughout my life. As a youngster, I had visited different churches and monasteries several times to find out more about Christianity. However, what came across to me was mostly dogmas and regulations and I couldn't perceive the Love and greatness of Christ. But now, while hearing Swami's words, I could feel Him and my heart was expanding.

On the following day, a *yagna* was organised. This is a ceremony where we could offer rice into the fire and, through this act of offering, surrender all our emotions, worries or wishes to the Divine. I felt very relieved after this gathering and the whole journey was joyful and blessed from the beginning until the end.

Later, my friend and I visited Swami several times more in Steffenshof.

On one such occasion, I met him in the small Christian chapel next to the *ashram*. While there, He showed me the icons of the saints painted by Him and His devotees. He told me that a *guru* and the form of God were very important for a seeker, and that only a few individuals reach God through His Cosmic Form.

He said, 'People need a form to focus upon, and you also need a form, and therefore I am here…'. I could understand the meaning behind some of His words immediately, and for some, I needed years to understand.

One day, I wanted to paint something for Swami and chose, as a subject, the newly created logo of His movement, which received the name '*Bhakti Marga*', the Path of Devotion. The logo was the sign of *om* with a cross and other religious symbols coming out of a lotus flower. I painted it with a special method which ended up turning into a beautiful meditation for me. The picture was framed and packed as a present for the next time I saw Him.

That summer, when I travelled with my friend to Germany, we visited the *ashram*. To our regret, Swami was not there but was in Greece. Not being able to see Him made me sad and I noticed my growing attachment to Him. The few residents of the *ashram* invited us to stay with them for the prayers. Even though Swami was not physically there, we could still strongly feel His presence.

I decided to leave my present for Him in the *ashram* without writing a note. The person who took it said she would place it in His room. During my subsequent visits to Steffenshof, I would look around to see if the picture was hanging somewhere at the *ashram*. Nearly a year later, I discovered it in the dining room, hanging above the serving table.

One evening, while having dinner with Swami, I thought to myself, 'He surely doesn't know who that picture is from.' After dinner, I went to get a cup of tea and happened to be standing right in front of the painting. I felt someone's presence behind me and when I turned to look, it was Swami standing there. He was looking straight at the painting and said aloud to Himself, 'Such a beautiful picture', and then walked away. When I heard this, I was stunned. It was a reply to my thought and I realised that He is well-aware of everything that is going on inside and outside of us.

*****

Each time I met Swami was special. He would reveal or teach me something, open some new opportunity, or evoke a state within myself which I had never experienced before. It was a saving grace to leave behind the turmoil of the world and to be in His presence; the worries would lose their importance, and I would feel secure and peaceful.

When someone's mere presence removes worldly attraction and awakens a longing for God, you know you have met a true Master.

He became like a father who would lovingly correct me when necessary or like a friend to whom I could entrust everything. Even if I was physically a few years older than Him, I felt like a child in front of an ageless Being.

Each time I was with him, He could appear different; sometimes he was as playful as a child and at other times as grand as God Himself; on some days he appeared very tall while on others he was of average height; at times he had dark skin and at other times, bright skin.

Little did I know what was coming next.

# Mauritius

In September 2005, my work contract was terminated. It did not come as a surprise as more and more of my focus was on Swami and less and less on my work. My friend and I took this as an opportunity to travel to Mauritius and visit Swami in his homeland. We spontaneously bought our flight tickets, booked a room, and set out for the small island in the Indian Ocean.

We arrived in Mauritius in the morning and that same day we went to the *ashram* in Quatre Bornes to meet him. To our great disappointment, a devotee who welcomed us told us that Swami had left the island just two days before. His departure was earlier than planned because He wanted to surprise His devotees back in Germany. It was truly unbelievable!

My first reaction was to fly back to Germany but, through my friend's comfort, she convinced me to stay. With a heavy heart we accepted the situation and tried to make the best of those two weeks. We regularly came to the *ashram*, which had a Hindu temple and a small, beautiful Christian chapel with multiple statues of Mother Mary. We visited several beautiful places on the island, went for walks along the beach, and tasted a variety of

Mauritian food. The atmosphere on the island was serene and people seemed to be much more relaxed, which helped us to slow down and enjoy our holiday.

One day, we visited Swami's home in Rose Hill where His father was still living. He welcomed us warmly inside the house and led us straight to Swami's childhood room. We gratefully followed him and were amazed by the sight and energy of the room. The whole space had a divine vibration; it was as though you entered some other dimension. The room was cool and fragrant with deities and pictures of saints and divinities hanging all over the walls, covered with *vibhuti* and *kumkum*. You could even see some self-manifested formations of OM and a cross on the wall plaster.

My friend fell on her knees and started crying. I left her alone and sat down for a short meditation while my entire body vibrated. When my friend composed herself, we sat silently observing all the wondrous details in the room. This was the place where many miracles and mystical experiences occurred during Swami's childhood. From His early years it was clear that He was not an ordinary child. He would spend every free minute praying, visiting temples and performing religious rituals; always living in the remembrance of God. At the age of five, His *guru*, Mahavatar Babaji, first appeared to Him. At the age of 14, He displayed the state of *samadhi*, a deep meditative state of complete absorption in the Divine.

Swami's father told us that his son's unique personality and realisation of the Divine began to attract people seeking His blessings and advice. After finishing His schooling, He began to follow His vocation as a spiritual teacher, leaving His home at the age of 16.

Before leaving, His father showed us Swami's photos from various events in His life. By looking at them, a deep realisation came to me: He was someone very close to me whom I already knew from the past. We left the house in silence and didn't talk much that evening. My friend only commented, 'Do you realise who He is?'

When the time for our departure came, we asked the devotees in the temple if there was anything we could take with us to the *ashram*, since our next destination was Steffenshof. They told us that when Swami left, He had too much luggage and had to leave two bags with statues there. We gladly agreed to take them with us on the flight and give them directly to Him.

At customs in the Munich airport, we were asked to open our suitcases. When they saw the two bags with the statues, they requested a value declaration. Neither of us ever thought to ask the devotees about the statues' value. We opened the bags and searched for some paper but couldn't find anything. As the police officer was insisting and would not let us go without a declaration, we eventually called the devotee in Mauritius. She, in turn, tried to reach Swami in Germany, but He was in prayers and was not available. Therefore, my friend and I decided to connect with Swami from inside and prayed. We silently repeated the *Gayatri-mantra* three times and asked Him for help.

The officials ultimately kept the goods with them and gave us twenty days to hand in the declaration. We signed a paper and left the customs office without the statues. When we were outside, we decided to look one last time in the bags. My friend had already searched several times while inside the airport. This time, to our surprise, she found a folded paper at the bottom. When she unfolded it, she saw it was the bill for the statues. It was truly a wonder, and I joked, 'Maybe it materialised?' We didn't have time to lose and rushed back to the customs officials. They rolled their eyes when they saw us but, since everything was accurate with the bill, they gave us back our goods and we then proceeded towards Steffenshof.

We arrived at the *ashram* on the next day. Swami was giving interviews and we were asked to wait in the temple. When He came out of the interview room, He approached us smilingly, and said 'I was thinking of you intensively yesterday. You were in Mauritius, weren't you?' We both nodded our heads while He called us inside His room. He asked us about our stay in Mauritius, what we were doing there, and how we liked the island. We mentioned the different places we had visited and people we had met. We told Him we had met someone who was also a Swami there. At that point He emphasised, 'You don't need to look for other *gurus* anymore. I am your *guru*. Actually, I am your *satguru*.'

After saying this, He materialised a cross pendant with green crystals for my friend and a beautiful ring with a red stone for me. We were at a loss for words as His presents were of a priceless value to us. When He looked at me, I felt so unworthy that I covered my face. I didn't know why this feeling came over me, but it was powerful and seemed to have some history behind it.

Eventually, He asked us about the statues. I briefly mentioned our adventure at the customs office. When I told Him that we had finally found the bill in the luggage, He interrupted me saying, 'The bill is with me. It was with the other bags.' I explained again, 'Swami, we found it.' He repeated, 'It is here. I carried it with me last time from Mauritius.' At last, I took the bill out of my purse and gave it to Him. He looked at it smiling and said in a pleased manner, 'The angels have done a good job; even the end sum was reduced!' I couldn't believe my ears and wanted to reassure myself,

'Swami, it was materialised?' He made a slight gesture of affirmation and asked us to go and join the prayers.

We left the room and sat down in the temple but, due to my great excitement, I couldn't concentrate. After the prayers, my friend and I stayed in silence a bit longer. Suddenly, people started rushing into the interview room we had just been in with Swami. Apparently, something special was happening there.

My curiosity got the best of me, and I eventually followed the crowd back to the interview room. In the now overcrowded room, Swami was sitting on His chair, holding in His hand a golden *lingam* which was freshly manifested out of his throat from His heart. Looking at all of us, He asked if we knew what it was. He then explained about the rare appearance of the *Hiranyagarbha-lingam*, the Soul of God and the seed of the whole Creation. It manifests on earth from time to time to bring balance on our planet and to uplift all of those who are in search of the Truth. The *lingam* was placed on the temple altar so that everyone could venerate it and receive its blessing.

This was, indeed, a day of miraculous wonders. As I lay down for bed that night, the impressions made from these experiences were still running through my mind and I couldn't sleep. The ring which Swami materialised for me felt as though it was 'alive', moving slightly around my finger and releasing some special vibration.

I had found my *satguru*, the most amazing and wondrous Being on Earth!

# The Dream

A cousin I grew up with in Serbia was having a wedding and I didn't want to miss it. I also saw going to the wedding as an opportunity for me to see my whole family. Even though I was in a busy period with my studies in Vienna, I managed to take a few days off. In order to be on time for the wedding, I travelled by car through the night and arrived in my hometown early the next morning. During that whole day we had the wedding celebration.

Late at night, I came back with my sister to our parents' house where she was living with her family and where I also had a room. Although we were living together for only a few years during our childhood, my sister and I still felt close to each other. However, when it came to the topic of spirituality, she simply couldn't follow. She often got upset and we had to change the topic.

That night she got upset and blamed me for neglecting the family for the sake of some *guru*. I tried to explain to her the role of a spiritual teacher but it just ended up creating an even bigger dispute between us. I felt offended and was considering leaving the house. I knew doing this would have created a bigger conflict and so I stayed. After all, I knew her character; she would calm down soon and everything would be okay the next day.

During that night, I had an exceptional dream: Some guards guided me to a place where I could meet Swami. He didn't look the same, but I knew that it was Him. He asked me if I would come with him to America. At first, I hesitated, considering my financial situation, but Swami responded, saying, 'I will give you the money'. I answered that this was not necessary and agreed that I would come. In the next moment, the whole space around us was luminous and then the dream suddenly ended.

When I woke up in the morning, I felt energised and was in a good mood. I remembered the dream clearly but didn't take it very seriously at the time, thinking that it was only a nice dream with Swami. However, when I came back to Austria, I realised that He was going on a tour to America for a few weeks. At this point, I reconsidered my dream as His invitation to come see Him. I checked the dates and venues of His tour, took some holiday, and booked my flight to California. Since everything happened spontaneously, during the flight a concern arose in me that Swami might not be pleased seeing me there. Whenever the concern would come up, I would remind myself of the dream and try to trust and relax.

From Los Angeles, I took the train to Encinitas, which was home to the Indian saint and *guru* Paramahansa Yogananda and is still the largest base of his spiritual movement. My first night there, I spent on the street but the next day I managed to find some simple and cheap accommodation in a town nearby the city.

Before Swami's upcoming Darshan in Encinitas, I went for a walk along the wide boulevard with palm trees and beautiful buildings. The weather was pleasantly warm with a mild ocean breeze. Along the way, I entered a few bookstores and passed along the information about the Darshan with Swami Vishwananda to those I met inside.

When I reached the Darshan hall, around a hundred people were already waiting for the program to begin. A devotee from Steffenshof greeted me and asked me to assist Swami with handing out *vibhuti* ash and rose petals during the Darshan. I very gladly agreed to help.

When Swami arrived, He welcomed me with the words, 'You have come', in a manner as though He expected me to come. During the Darshan I was sitting close to Him and, to my surprise, noticed tears in His eyes. I wondered why He would cry and thought to myself that He might be sad about the state of humans and the world, in general.

After the Darshan I approached and asked Him about it, but He only said, 'I didn't cry. Maybe the tears came because of the strong light. When I cry, the tears are rolling from the front of my face.' He then called an American lady and asked her to take me with her to Rancho Mirage in a few days, where He would have His next event.

I left the Darshan Hall with strange emotions inside of me and found myself upset without any obvious reason. When I reached the bus station of Encinitas, I found there was no public transportation running any longer and so I stayed another night awake in a restaurant.

The following two days, I spent in silence, walking along the beach, resting, and reading. On the third day, together with the American lady, I travelled by car to the Californian desert to meet Swami again. During the trip, we talked about our experiences, how we met Swami, His miracles and about His previous incarnations.

When we arrived, we found our destination to be a beautiful green oasis in the middle of the desert. Swami was giving interviews in a private house and we went straight there for a meeting.

When He came out of His room to greet us, I quickly took the opportunity to mention my dream. When I began with, 'Swami, I had a dream…', He interrupted me softly, saying, 'I know, we will talk later.'

Shortly thereafter, He called me into His room and I finally had the chance to ask, 'Swami why have you called me to America? Is it something special?' He smiled and emphasised, 'Each time it is something special!' He then asked about my general well-being, about Austria, and then if I would wish to have a family, to marry and have children or not. I was surprised about this last question and wondered why He would ask such things. After a short moment of silence, I replied, 'Both ways are ok. What do you think, what is better for me?' He looked at me and said, 'I know your soul, but I don't know your mind. Think about it and tell me tomorrow.' He took my ring and held it for a while and then stood up and left.

I wanted to stay in the room to meditate on His words when He came back and called me for dinner. I was not a self-confident person and hesitated to join, but He pulled me to the dining room. He told me to sit next to Him at the table, where ten people were sitting, freely dining and conversing, while I remained shy and silent.

I was invited to stay overnight in a hotel with His devotees and when I left after the dinner, the interview conversation played back in my mind. I was lost in thought and completely missed the hotel when it was right in front of my face. When I finally reached there, my two roommates were worried about me. To one of them, I mentioned my conversation with Swami and expressed my confusion about its meaning. Usually, I would understand Swami's indirect hints, but this time it was different. The devotee excused herself, as she had to continue working on preparations for initiations on the following day. When she mentioned the initiations, I asked a few more questions about it. Since she was busy, she postponed the answers for later. I had heard that Swami initiated some of His devotees at the Steffenshof ashram into monastics, but I thought that this had been a one-time event. Anyway, it had been an intense day and I instantly fell asleep despite having so many unanswered questions swirling through my mind.

The desert sun woke me up early in the morning and I went to the balcony to do some *yoga* practice. Everything was calm, with artificially beautiful nature, many palm trees and a green golf course in front of the hotel. After the exercises, I contemplated on Swami's words from the day before, took a pen and paper and started writing.

Firstly, I asked myself about the central focus of my life, which undoubtedly was God. I had already been married and lived the worldly life, yet something was still missing. Even if I would have a husband and children, the longing for God would always be there. Swami was my role model and I wished to follow His footsteps. He was a *sannyasin* (renunciate) and at the same time He was full of life, inspiring, enlightened and free like a bird.

At this point, it crossed my mind that He might really have called me for initiation and that it was going to happen that day. This would have been an amazing divine play, arranged by a Master, but I still was not sure. If He had, indeed, called me to become a monastic, that would mean that I was capable of it. Ultimately, He knew my soul better than I did!

Throughout the morning, it became crystal clear to me that it *was* His call, and I impatiently waited to get it confirmed by Him.

On the way to Swami's place, my roommate explained the meaning of *brahmacharya* initiation and the vow of obedience, simplicity and celibacy which one takes. As soon as we arrived at the house, I sought Swami to continue our conversation from the day before. I approached Him with the question, 'I heard today is an initiation, will you also initiate me?'

Without being surprised, He asked, 'Do you want it?'

I determinedly said, 'Yes.'

'Do you know what it means?', He asked further, and I replied with slightly less resolution, 'Yes.'

'Good. I will initiate you today,' He said.

I was delighted and took advantage of this moment to verify His call. 'Was this the reason you called me in a dream to come?'

He smiled charmingly and said, 'Yes.'

I looked at Him and wondered at how amazing He was. He had enacted this whole divine play but gave me the freedom to decide for myself, all the while, leading me to the realisation from within. A day before, I didn't understand anything, and then, suddenly, different puzzle pieces all came together and revealed the complete picture. How blessed was this moment of revelation!

# The Initiation

It is often said that the best moments in our life come when we least expect them. On March 18, 2006, I experienced one of my life's greatest moments with my 'new birth' as a *brahmacharini*, a Hindu nun.

About ten people gathered for the initiation ceremony held in the house where Swami was staying. Upon arriving, I was surprised to see that the American lady I had travelled with was also there to receive initiation. It seemed that no one knew exactly what was going to take place. When the process of the ceremony was explained, I was excited but also a bit concerned that I was going to make some mistakes. I concluded that the best way to approach the experience was to follow what others were doing and just 'go with the flow'.

The first part of our initiation was the purification. As part of this, Swami cut a few stands of our hair, symbolising our material detachment. He then poured turmeric water over our heads, drenching our clothes in the dark-yellow colour and almost inaudibly pronounced, 'Your *karma* is finished.' Once we changed into clean, white clothes, the next step of our initiation was to be a part of a *yagna*. After the *yagna*, it was time to take the *brahmacharya* vow and to receive a spiritual name which carries a specific vibration and has certain qualities that are beneficial for us. I was resistant to being given a typical Hindu name and hoped to receive a Christian spiritual name or, at the very least, one that didn't sound strange.

One by one, we approached Swami in a separate room where, kneeling in front of Him, we read aloud our vow. We declared that we accept Him as our *satguru* and surrender to Him to our level best, trusting that He will lead us to our final destination. To my embarrassment, I had difficulty pronouncing several English words, but Swami didn't seem to care about it and blessed me by placing His hand on my head. He painted a Vaishnava *tilak* on my forehead, as a constant reminder of God, and gave me the spiritual name, 'Triambhakeshwari'.

It could have been a very solemn moment if only my mind hadn't rebelled after hearing such a long and 'typical' Hindu name. As I tried to hide my disappointment, Swami, who from that time on was 'Guruji' for me, mentioned something about my new name's meaning. I couldn't understand what He said as my thoughts were running after ideas of how to shorten it and make it sound more ordinary.

Shortly after finishing the initiation, several people informed me that my *tilak* looked like a cross on my forehead. It was so unusual that Guruji came and investigated the red *kumkum* line Himself (which, in the *Vaishnava* tradition, represents Maha-Lakshmi) running down through my forehead wrinkle, creating the sign of the cross.

After taking some photos with Guruji, we prepared lunch together. As in the times before, I was shy and insecure as to how to behave in His presence.

In the afternoon, I went for a walk in the surrounding area. It was a modern residential complex with large, green spaces. The air, coming from the nearby mountains, was fresh and feelings of freedom and contentment started to well up from somewhere inside of me. There were no emotions or thoughts, only peace and quietness. I felt elevated, safe and carried by the Divine. Everything was in harmony around me, and I was simply the observer.

Before Guruji departed for Maui, He asked me about my plans for the next days. I intended to visit a friend, but Guruji arranged for me to stay with a devotee in Los Angeles until my departure to Europe. He told me that, when Bhakti Marga acquired a bigger *ashram*, I could come live there. 'Maybe in one and a half years', he said. This possibility was pleasing, and it corresponded perfectly with my schooling since I was just finishing the first year of my studies and had two more years to go until I received my diploma.

Just as Guruji had arranged, the next three days I spent with a devotee in L.A. While there, I maintained that same, undisturbed inner state, simply observing and not being affected by the world around me.

On the second night, I had another significant dream. In it, it was shown that I had been elevated to a certain state of consciousness through the previous initiation but I understood that it would be difficult to retain that state due to my agitated mind.

From the third day after my initiation, emotions once again started to arise within me, and thoughts began running all through my mind. My state of inner peace and quietness was slowly dissipating.

Once back in Austria, I felt that my life had forever changed, and that Guruji's blessing was with me in all my activities. I started wearing brown and less attractive clothes according to the *brahmacharya* guidelines and, overall, felt more satisfied. The only work I still had was a short-term job for an NGO helping victims of human trafficking. The rest of the time was reserved for my studies and spirituality.

# The Call to the Ashram

A few weeks later, after Guruji had come back from America, another public event took place with a *yagna* and Darshan. The venue was located in a beautiful forest on the edge of Basel in Germany. My friend and I drove from Austria and arrived just in time for the *yagna*.

People from different countries were participating and everyone wanted to be close to Guruji. When the *yagna* started, He called all *brahmacharis* to do the offering together. As a few of us gathered, I felt pride arising inside of me. Even without wanting it, it was there.

During the *yagna*, Guruji was scolding a devotee. This was the first time that I saw Him being strict. I didn't know what that person had done, but I was afraid that He might be strict with me too. My concern was that I would not be able to handle His scolding.

After the *yagna*, I stayed outside to meditate around the *kund* and to enjoy the blessing of the ceremony. Everyone else went inside the building for a meal. While outside, it passed through my mind that Guruji might be together with all of them, yet I preferred to stay there alone. 'Maybe He didn't even notice me', I thought to myself. With this in mind, I heard some people talking close by. When I looked up at them, I saw Guruji standing on the balcony by Himself, observing me. I felt embarrassed and realised how easily one can imagine things and believe them to be true.

The program continued in the evening, where Guruji greeted us. He personally inquired with me how the *brahmacharya* life was. After the initiation, I wanted to live a more withdrawn life and considered moving away from Vienna to the quieter countryside. I took the opportunity to tell Guruji about it. After hearing it, he repeated wonderingly, 'You want to move to the *ashram*?'

I was perplexed for a moment, as this was not at all what I had said. Keeping in mind that a Master would never say something without a reason, I tried to understand the deeper message behind His question. Eventually I asked Him, 'Would it be good for me to move to the *ashram*?' He thought for a short while and said, 'But you still have your job there.' With that, our conversation ended but that night, I had a dream that my path would soon lead towards an *ashram* life.

After coming back home from the event, it became an ever-increasing inner call. In the beginning, I tried not to think about it much and to stay focused on my studies in which I had invested an enormous amount of time and effort. The study program was going well, and I wanted to graduate.

Furthermore, I didn't like the idea of returning to Germany and hoped that the bigger *ashram*, which Bhakti Marga would someday obtain, would be in another country, preferably on the seaside.

However, the inner call came again and again until I had another dream with Guruji. In this dream, He clearly showed me that the *ashram* life would be beneficial, though not easy for me. His conclusion with me was, 'It's on you to decide.'

After that dream, I had the needed clarity within myself to make the decision to close everything in Austria and move to the *ashram* in Germany. I was given the realisation that the *satguru*, His presence, wisdom, and teaching cannot be compared to any worldly education or graduation. I didn't want to miss the rare opportunity to learn directly from the Master.

The next time I went to the *ashram* for a public event with Guruji, I approached Him saying, 'Guruji, I have decided to come.' Since He told me in a dream that it was for me to decide to live in the *ashram* or not, I considered it appropriate to inform Him of my decision.

He looked at me enquiringly, 'You have decided to come here for this event?'

'No', I replied, 'to come and live here'.

He thought for a while and said, 'Ok. Next month the room above will be free. You can move in there.' It was a speedy agreement between us and the plan was made to move to the *ashram* in three months.

Before that, however, one more trip awaited me: Guruji's Darshan Tour through Croatia, Serbia, Hungary and Austria. Since I was responsible for organising the Darshan in Belgrade, I had the good fortune to be on that tour with Guruji and some of His devotees. Our meeting point was in Croatia, in a small town dedicated to Mother Mary. I arrived directly from Austria by car and met the group there.

Guruji liked Christian Orthodoxy and, since Montenegro and Serbia are Orthodox countries, I had already planned a tour to different churches and monasteries.

In Croatia, close to the town where we were staying, was a well-known Orthodox monastery. I suggested to Guruji that we go there with the group. He agreed to go but only with one other person and myself.

We left early in the morning, expecting a one-hour drive but, due to the narrow roads, it took much longer. On the way, I asked Guruji about the rumour that Jesus had been in India. He answered that John the Baptist had travelled to India and took the ceremonies of bathing in the Ganges and spiritual initiation as inspiration for baptisms in the Jordan River.

When we arrived at the monastery, the monks there informed us that a liturgy service with a bishop was being conducted in the nearby village, commemorating Saint Prokopios. We drove there and found a small, half-empty church with several priests and monks conducting the service. The three of us stood at the back of the church, observing the ceremony, while people looked at us curiously.

In the *sanctorum*, I noticed a priest singing the liturgy very merrily. My impression was that he was drunk. When I caught myself with such thoughts, I felt embarrassed in front of Guruji, knowing He was able to read my mind.

When the time for the Holy Communion came, Guruji made a sign to the devotee and I indicating that we should partake. The moment we queued up, we were both questioned by a monk: the other devotee because he was French, and me because I had a nose piercing.

'Are you Orthodox?', the monk asked me.

'Yes', I replied.

He turned towards the clergy exclaiming, 'She claims to be Orthodox and has a piercing in her nose!'

It was embarrassing, especially because Guruji was observing the scene. However, I remained in the queue. When my turn came to receive communion, the 'merry' priest was very friendly and I tried, again, to suppress the thought that he was drunk. I returned to our place and took shelter behind Guruji. He inquired what the monk had asked me and was puzzled about the incident. He later approached and talked to that particular monk.

Since one part of the ceremony was the procession, we circled the outside of the church. While going around it, I asked Guruji, 'If the service is performed by someone who is not sincere, is the ceremony working?' Guruji replied, 'Even if a criminal in a prison calls the Holy Spirit, the moment he calls, It (the Holy Spirit) is there'. At the end of His reply, He stated that, 'If people would feel more love at these places (meaning the churches), they would come.'

We entered the church again and before our departure, the 'interrogating' monk bade us a polite farewell.

In the car on the way back, Guruji remarked, 'The priest seemed to be drunk.'
We all laughed, and I was relieved that I was not the only one seeing it. Guruji concluded with the words, 'You understand now why I didn't want to bring the whole group there.'

In the following days, we visited various holy sites; Medjugorje in Herzegovina, St. Basil of Ostrog in Montenegro, St. Peter of Kornish and Zica Monastery in Serbia. Guruji was enjoying these places. Several times I caught a beautiful sight of Him being lost in a prayer or communion with the Divine. He, Himself, looked like a holy icon.

His relationship with the saints was remarkable. He has often stated that they are His good friends. He disclosed that His favourite was the wonderworker and speedy helper, St. Nicholas. When I asked why He preferred the Orthodox church, He replied, 'Because it is more honest.'

During our stay in Medjugorje, I faced a situation of emotional distress. We were sitting at the lunch table, when suddenly my mind became very disturbed. I didn't want to let it show and went to the rest room to compose myself. Guruji must have noticed because, when I came back to the table, He called me to sit next to Him. I sat at His table and pretended nothing had happened. He offered me some food from His plate but, as I had plenty of food on my own, I refused. Other devotees wondered about my behaviour and explained the meaning of *Maha-prasad*, the blessed food, whereupon I took a little bit of it.

After lunch, our group visited the main church of Medjugorje. Guruji was standing in the front while I stayed at the back, mixing in with the crowds and intensively praying for help. Without any visible reason, He turned and looked among the crowd as if searching for someone. When He saw me, He looked at me for a while, as if to confirm that He had heard my prayer. The affliction eventually vanished and everything within me was fine again. It was a mystery to me why this unexplained emotional distress happened and why I could not control myself better in those moments.

While passing through Montenegro, a local told me about a monastery where an elder, who was considered a saint, was living. I told Guruji about this and He agreed that we would all go there to visit him. Since the monastery was at a remote place along a narrow mountain road, we reached there after hours of driving. A few nuns welcomed us but, to our regret, the elder wasn't there. I had dearly wished to see the meeting between the elder and Guruji; to witness two saints greeting each other. In my imagination, I saw the elder becoming lost in Guruji's eyes or even resting in his embrace.

In the meantime, we visited the church and had a long conversation with the nuns. Just shortly before our departure, the elder arrived. I was glad that the meeting eventually worked out. We greeted the elder in a respectful way and sat down for a conversation in front of the church. To my utter astonishment, he didn't notice Guruji. To my even greater disappointment, he started talking about the exclusivity of Orthodoxy and the Masons.

While I was translating, I looked over at Guruji a few times, making a sign with my eyes, expressing, 'Let us leave from here', but he seemed to be interested in the conversation and ignored my signals.

After the meeting, Guruji stated that the elder was, indeed, a saintly person. From this comment, I understood that there must exist different levels of sainthood and realisation. It seemed that not all saints were fully realised beings. Years later, Guruji explained the difference between self-realisation and God-realisation and that He does not 'show Himself' to everyone.

Our journey continued through Serbia, where at one point, my family came to greet Guruji. My young nieces welcomed Him in traditional Serbian dress and my mother prepared traditional food. Even my father and grandfather came to meet us. We had a picnic together in a monastery courtyard and afterwards, moved on towards Belgrade.

In Belgrade, the Darshan was beautiful, with more than three hundred people receiving Guruji's blessing. Many were deeply touched by His presence and several of them became His followers.

From Serbia, our journey continued to Hungary and Austria. After the Darshan in Vienna, Guruji went back to Germany while I stayed in order to pack and prepare for the next step in my life: the *ashram* life.

# The Early Ashram Life

I moved to the *ashram* in Steffenshof at the end of August 2006. The *ashram* had several buildings and one of them was the *brahmacharini* house, where around 6 *matajis* (women) lived together. My small room was on the first floor.

The house had a big living room, where Guruji often spent His time. Next to the house, was another building where Bhakti Marga had an office, a small church, and where Guruji had His room. Opposite to it, was the temple, and above the temple were the dining and sleeping areas for guests. Altogether, the *ashram* had around fifteen residents of varying ages, backgrounds and nationalities. The duties were shared. My *seva* (duty) was to welcome the guests and to take care of the entire guest area.

Our daily program consisted of morning and evening prayers for around forty minutes, the morning *yagna* in a tipi tent next to the temple, and a guided meditation by Guruji at noon.

Our main deities (*murtis*) were Maha-Vishnu, Maha-Lakshmi, and Mahavatar Babaji, to whom daily *puja* was performed. On Sundays, there was *maha-abishekam*, where the deities were bathed, clothed and worshipped. All of the residents were *pujaris* (those responsible for deity care and worship) and performed the ceremonies on a rotation.

We learned how to perform *puja*, *abhishekam* and *yagna*, to sing *bhajans* and to chant the *mantras*. We also learned Christian prayers, sang akathists in the church and painted icons.

In the beginning, I was busy with memorising the different ceremonies, hymns and prayers, sometimes struggling with Sanskrit. I was familiar with most of the deities, but I needed some time to familiarise myself with Narasimha, a half-lion and half-man incarnation. My amazement was that after all those ceremonies, I felt more peaceful.

Guruji spent most of His time in the *ashram*, but He was also travelling a lot.

From time to time He would call us for a meeting to give us instructions about *brahmacharya* and the *ashram* life.

The majority of us were still quite young. Often, one could observe a *brahmachari* (man) spending a lot of time with some of the *brahmacharinis* (women), which was a danger for the monastic life. Guruji advised us not to spend unnecessary time with the opposite gender, to take our meals in silence, and, in general, to talk less and not to gossip. He told us to spend one day a week in silence, to take half an hour every day to sit and analyse our behaviour, not to judge and to give others space and time for their own development.

He reminded us to be kind-hearted to people, emphasising that 'a smile didn't cost anything', and not to expect gratitude for our *seva*. Also, the gifts we happen to receive should be shared with everyone. What was not to be shared with others were our problems and He asked that we approach Him with our concerns.

He also wanted us to wear a simple brown robe during our *seva* time and a white long skirt or sari during the prayers. Guruji explained that brown was a neutral colour, protecting and grounding, while white stood for purity.

At first, He wanted us to address each other with 'brother' and 'sister', but he changed it later to, '*prabhu*' and '*mataji*'. He advised us not to embrace other people, especially when dealing with the opposite gender, except for our closest family.

Since our *brahmacharya* initiation was a new birth, Guruji told us to celebrate this date as our birthday. In general, He emphasised obedience, humility, and simplicity.

Guruji often let us work out and decide things among ourselves, omnisciently holding the whole process. Most things developed smoothly but sometimes, due to different characters and opinions, Guruji had to intervene.

Owing to the fact that He was often in our living room, we were occasionally able to ask Guruji some questions or He would freely reveal some mystery about God or about Himself. In general, however, He did not want the residents to hang around Him, especially during prayer time. After our *seva* times, in the evenings we could be with Him in the room, sitting around the table in silence, sometimes following the conversation or helping with something.

On one occasion Guruji gave everyone in the *ashram* a personal *mantra*. Sometime later we received from Him the sacred *mantra* '*om namo narayanaya*' ('I salute the Lord, in whom all things abide and who abides in all things'). He explained that this was the highest *mantra* which was kept secret and given only through initiation for thousands of years. It contains all other *mantras* and represents the means to salvation, since the chanting of the Divine Names is the best path to liberation in the modern age.

For us, the *mantra* served to calm and focus our agitated minds, which obviously still needed purification!

* * * * *

By moving to the *ashram*, I expected to have a closer relationship with Guruji and to be able to spend more personal time with Him. This did not turn out to be the case. He rarely talked to me; sometimes He even ignored me.

Around two months after my arrival, different kinds of negativity started to arise in me. On some days, I was in such a poor mood that it was impossible to be around Guruji; I would start judging, comparing myself with others or being envious. There was a deep impression that He didn't care about me, which created a bigger and more painful distance to Him. I couldn't be in His presence when I knew my negative thoughts and feelings would be obvious since nothing is hidden from Him.

When I couldn't bear it any longer, I took courage to approach Him and ask for help. He encouraged me saying, 'It's normal that you feel like this. Around Me everything is sped up and comes to the surface quicker. What one would need to work out in several lives, around Me can happen in only a few years.'

He also said that this was one of the reasons why He frequently travelled; we simply would not be able to handle all the internal issues that would arise by being in His continual presence.

His advice was always nectar for my soul and would leave me feeling centred and strengthened again. The only problem was that, after some time, the mind would find some other reason to rebel again. I would feel hurt or not fairly treated or ignored. The list of trivialities could go on and on.

During one such period, I observed how Guruji had closer relationships with other people, spending time, joking and singing with them. Yet, with me, He appeared to be serious and distant. One day, I happened to meet Him in the kitchen and took the courage to complain about it, saying, 'Guruji, I have the feeling that you are giving more attention to some people.' He turned to me with His big, black eyes. I immediately regretted saying this, but it was too late. With a strict voice, He questioned me, 'Are you accusing me of favouring some people?' There was no time to answer because He was like a volcano, which was burning my ego right on the spot. 'You think only of yourself! It's egoistic. It's not about what you feel, it is about your thinking; you have to divert it!'

I was frozen and for a moment, even my breath stopped.

His voice became a little bit softer, and He continued, 'If I pay more attention to others it is because they need it, the soul needs it, and when the soul doesn't need it anymore, I leave! You should be happy when I am with other people!'

As He was planning to travel to Serbia on His next trip, He added, 'Do you think because you come from Serbia, I need to take you with me? With such thinking, I don't feel free. I will not take you. You make a slave out of yourself, divert such thoughts!'

This was the first time that Guruji was strict with me and, at that moment, I just wanted to disappear. However, I was aware that God didn't want me to run away but to learn something from it and to transform some of my deep-seated patterns.

I went to my room and the only thing I could do was to lie in bed and repeat my *mantra*. A huge pain spread throughout my body. I tried not to think but just breath and accept the present moment. What Guruji was teaching me was clear, but those patterns were so deep and strong, that I easily became their victim. It was difficult to control the mind, especially in His presence.

For the remainder of that day and the next, I didn't leave my room. On the evening of the second day, another devotee knocked on my door and told me that Guruji was asking about me. I came silently to the living room where He and some other devotees were sitting at the table. When He saw me, He commented, 'You are alive', and I answered, 'Yes', remaining silent for the rest of the evening.

Throughout the years, it became evident to me that Guruji could be very strict in order to correct us and remove the ignorance, but the moment we realised our mistake and made the effort to rectify it, He would act as though nothing had ever happened.

A few weeks later while we were sitting together in the kitchen, He started talking about saints and monasteries. He told me that soon He would be travelling to Serbia and that I could, in fact, come with Him!

To learn directly from the Master was certainly the best thing that could have ever happened to me, but definitely not the easiest for the ego.

## Guruji's Teaching

Guruji teaches *bhakti*: true love and devotion. *Bhakti* doesn't depend on any religion, but on the intensity of one's love for God and the quality of the relationship with Him. God is not exclusive to any religion, but rather religion needs to support us with our spiritual goal of attaining Him. There is only One God, the Source and the Indweller of all existence, seated deep inside everyone's heart, patiently waiting for us to turn to Him. He can be called by many different names, but what matters is the love and servitude we cultivate during our lifetime towards Him and His whole creation.

Guruji's mission is to open the hearts of human beings and awaken the Divine Love present within them. He helps people realise their true identity and reunite with their divine nature.

In the following years, Guruji continued initiating His followers into Vaishnava *brahmacharyas* (as monks and nuns) and *jal brahmacharya* (as devotees who still had worldly duties). Vaishnavism is one of the major traditions within the broader Vedic, or Hindu, spiritual culture. To be a Vaishnava is not just a belief, but a state of consciousness and personification of the highest human values, such as unconditional love, humility and surrender.

A true Vaishnava feels the pain of others and helps those who are in misery. He respects the entire world, does not disparage anyone, and keeps his words, actions, and thoughts pure. He sees all equally. He is detached from the world and firmly attached to God and His Name. He has forsaken greed and deceit and stays far away from desire and anger.

Anyone with these qualities, regardless of religion, caste and creed, is dear to God and will attain Him!

Bhakti Marga follows the eternal principles of *Sanatana-dharma*, 'The Eternal Religion or Path' on which Vedic culture and Hinduism is based. Some of the main points of *Sanatana-dharma* are:

*Atma*: the existence of an immortal Self
*Brahma:* the Supreme Being (God)
*Shrishti*: the universal cycle of creation and destruction
*Samsara*: the evolution back to God through rebirth
*Karma*: the moral law of cause and effect
*Dharma*: the duty, right living, ethics, and morals
*Moksha*: the liberation from *samsara* for all conscious beings

In *Bhagavad Gita*, the process of creation and the immanence of God is precisely described; the different elements of the material and spiritual nature *(prakriti* and *purusha),* as well as the Supreme realm *(vaikuntha)* and the transcendency of God.

In Vaishnavism, Maha-Vishnu (Narayana) and His incarnations, such as Rama, Krishna, and Narasimha are worshipped as the Supreme Being, the Creator of everything and the saviour of souls from the cycle of birth and death. Considering Christ as one such incarnation on Earth, Hinduism is very accepting of Christianity, as well as all other religions.

The main practices of Bhakti tradition include devotional singing and the worship of murtis. Through a process known as *Prana Pratistha*, the Divine is invoked into a statue which becomes the living manifestation of God, a *murti*. In doing so, God is not limited by the form of deity (since He is present everywhere and inside every person), but by worshipping the deity, the loving relationship to God awakens. As a result, the *murti* is cared for, bathed, dressed and glorified.

Guruji actively encourages people to become vegetarians (or vegans) for spiritual, health, sociological and moral reasons. He often speaks of the cruelty and horrors of the meat industry in which living sentient beings are farmed and then slaughtered unnecessarily for the pleasure of human beings. He states that, 'A healthy body comes from the food that you eat. The healthy food you eat also makes your mind healthy. If your mind is healthy, your spiritual path will also be healthy.'

In previous times and in some cases, eating meat was a necessity to survive. However, today, living a healthy vegetarian lifestyle is easily accomplished, as there is a choice and means by which to live without participating in the killing of animals.

In this way, Guruji was the perfect teacher for me. I liked the principles of *Sanatana-dharma*, and at the same time, resonated with Christ and His blessed saints.

Guruji was my inspiration and deepened my understanding of Christianity. He showed His ultimate proximity to Christ. Just in the ways He talked about Christ's life and teachings, a higher perspective would be revealed.

I also came to realise that the same great Masters repeatedly incarnate into different religions to play significant roles for the benefit of humanity. Most importantly I understood that Guruji Himself, is an enlightened Being, present on Earth, doing everything as an expression of Love and sacrifice.

Throughout the years, Guruji has given a great variety of discourses with inspiring stories about God, His *avatars* (main incarnations) and saints. He has answered innumerable questions and, in doing so, has led us to direct experiences of an inner understanding. That understanding can awaken the Love of God in each of us. He often points out that things are happening by God's grace, but it is on us to give the best effort.

At some point, Guruji gave us the task to study the *Bhagavad Gita*, the *Srimad Bhagavatam* and the *Bible*, and to compare the lives and teachings of Krishna and Christ. He asked us to write about it and to present Him the work in due course of time.

He mentioned several times that He would soon provide a technique which would help focus and calm the mind, and in turn, would help elevate us on our spiritual path. And in March 2007, Guruji gave Bhakti Kriya - now Atma Kriya Yoga - together with OM Healing (OM Chanting), the ancient group healing practice, to the world. It was an amazing grace to receive this ancient and sacred technique of *yoga*, and even more precious receiving it directly from Him during a two-week retreat.

Throughout the centuries, Mahavatar Babaji, Guruji's teacher, who agreed to remain in a physical body to protect and oversee the long-term spiritual evolution of mankind and our planet, has given various types of *Kriya Yoga* through different Masters and *gurus* as a means for self-realisation. Atma Kriya Yoga was given by Mahavatar Babaji and Guruji with the focus on *bhakti*. The Shaktipat (transmitting of spiritual energy), Their blessing and grace, were given as a means for God-realisation.

The course took place in the *ashram* temple with around fifty students, which Guruji chose from all over the world. At first, He gave theoretical information, showed us the exercises and let us practise for some time or days. In between, he narrated many inspiring stories about *bhakti* and sang *bhajans*.

In connection with one exercise, He even gave us a drop of self-manifested *amrit*, the divine nectar, into our mouths. At the end, we received the Shaktipat initiation from Him, where I felt that He unlocked some very high potency within us.

Guruji said that many of us were practising *Kriya Yoga* in our past lives and that this fact would contribute to our progress with Atma Kriya Yoga, which, all together, has five levels or initiations. For most of us, it was the practice our souls were longing for; a link to bring us closer to the goal of life.

* * * * *

From time-to-time, Guruji's teaching would take a slightly new course and emphasis. It seemed that when we were ready, He opened new horizons for us, new opportunities and new revelations.

Early in the summer of 2007, some of us went with Guruji to Croatia for a Darshan in Split. This trip turned out to be one of those times when His mission took on another dimension and I was lucky enough to witness it.

We had accommodation together with the Croatian devotees in an apartment house close to the sea. One night, Guruji was ecstatically singing together with the whole group until very late. By thc time the gathering ended, it was three in the morning. Together, with another devotee, I left for a short walk along the beach before going to sleep.

As we were walking, a bright light suddenly illuminated the whole sky. I stopped and looked around to find where the light was coming from. I found the sky was clear and full of stars. It was obvious that it was not a lightning bolt or fireworks as there were no loud sounds accompanying the light.

As far as we could tell, there was no explanation. We continued walking and arrived back at our apartment house, where another devotee was standing on the beach. She described to us how she had been down on the beach, freely dancing with a cushion and, only at the end of her dancing, noticed that Guruji had been on the balcony observing her. The story ended there, and I didn't think any more about it.

When we came back to Germany, Guruji called all the residents to gather outside on the grass field. He started singing *bhajans* and told us to sing joyfully with raised hands while dancing in a circle. This was something new, but we followed and enjoyed it.

After the daily prayers on the following day, Guruji gave a *satsang* (discourse). He started talking about His time in Croatia. He narrated that one night while He was standing on the balcony, He observed a devotee on the beach, dancing with a cushion like mad. 'As I was observing her, I thought to myself, maybe this is what God wants, to dance and to be mad for Him.' He continued, 'At that moment, a bright light illumined the whole sky. It was the confirmation.'

Immediately upon hearing this, I remembered and understood the incident with the light.

After the *satsang*, I quietly approached Guruji, saying, 'I also saw the light.'

'Really?', He wondered, 'What did you think that it was?'.

I shrugged my shoulders, not knowing what to say. Guruji turned to another person who was behind Him, and said, 'She also saw the light!'

From that time on, Guruji started inviting people to dance for God, and He Himself was more and more often seen singing and dancing ecstatically.

# The Wonders

After meeting Guruji, life became full of wonders. From the very beginning, His devotees were blessed to witness numerous miracles around Him. Some of His earliest miracles were the materialisations of jewellery, *vibhuti* and deities, manifestations of *Hiranyagarbha* and *Shiva-lingams*, divine apparitions and fragrances, or the pouring out of myrrh oil, *amrit* and *vibhuti* from icons, pictures, statues or deities. Guruji carried out all these acts with the utmost humility. Everything He did, and does, is for the spiritual upliftment of people and the world. He doesn't need anything for Himself as He is already complete in Himself.

Every miracle Guruji performs has its own story and a unique meaning behind it. With regards to jewellery materialisations, He explained that it is a gift from God, given to a person with a certain purpose. The material, colour, stone and shape all have a deeper meaning and a positive effect upon the person who wears it. Once that purpose is fulfilled, the jewellery might break, get lost or miraculously disappear. Some people have gotten a chain, others a pendant and some have even received a deity manifested directly out of Guruji's heart.

*****

Most of the residents at that time already had a *Shiva-lingam* and jewellery manifested by Guruji. As mentioned earlier, I had received a ring. As human nature is intrinsically greedy, I also wanted a *Shiva-lingam* and another ring.

As a result, I had two dreams in connection with this desire. In the first one, I was shown that people were receiving materialised rings as a support to overcome a particular obstacle in life. Once the problem had been overcome, they might receive another ring as further support. In my case, it was shown that my ring covers everything and that I would not receive another one.

In the second dream, it was revealed that I actually had a *lingam* underneath my skin, therefore, there was no need to be given another one.

*****

In the small church in Steffenshof, we had an icon of Mother Mary with Jesus, painted by one of Guruji's devotees. Above the icon, an oil lamp would burn throughout the day. At that time, it was my duty to collect, filter and pour the remaining oil from the lamp into small bottles to be distributed.

One day, a resident noticed that the icon itself was pouring out a fragrant 'myrrh oil', which was spreading a beautiful, uplifting scent around the whole area. It came from the faces of Mary and Jesus, flowed down the icon, and dropped onto the floor. The amount of oil became so profuse, that one of the devotees constructed an apparatus that collected and poured the oil into a glass container.

As I was in charge of collecting the oil from the oil lamps, the glass with the self-manifested myrrh oil ended up in my room. Guruji told us to mix it together with the oil from the oil lamps and give it to people as a blessing. Since the oil was in my care, I decided to taste a drop: it was a strong essence with a divine scent, similar to a rose. After several days, the myrrh oil suddenly stopped pouring from the icon. Some devotees heard Guruji say that it was because someone had touched the icon.

Over the next few years, it frequently happened that icons spontaneously started pouring this miraculous myrrh oil.

* * * * *

One day, shortly before a trip to Serbia, my mother came to the *ashram* for an interview with Guruji. He called both of us to the church and I used the opportunity to ask Him to bless my two self-painted icons. Even though they were not expertly painted, Guruji liked them and placed them for a while on the main altar in the *sanctorum*. On one of them, He Himself had helped with, by painting Christ's hair.

After the interview, Guruji left for prayers while my mother and I stayed in the church. When the time came for us to leave for the airport, I couldn't enter the Sanctorum to take the icons. I went to the temple to call Guruji, but since He was singing, I asked another *swami* to come and take them for me.

When the *swami* picked them up from the altar, he noticed some oil on the icon of Christ I had painted. We wondered about it for a moment, but since I was in a hurry, I took the icon, covered it with a t-shirt, and squeezed it into my suitcase.

Arriving at my friend's place in Belgrade, I took the icon out and then put the t-shirt on. Immediately, a divine scent spread all around and I realised that it was the myrrh oil, which had come out of Christ's head (hair). It obviously happened as a result of Guruji having blessed it.

I was sorry for my carelessness of placing it in the suitcase without due respect. The myrrh didn't continue pouring, but Christ remained very present in that icon.

* * * * *

When the first followers from Poland came to the *ashram* to meet Guruji, He was playfully manifesting *vibhuti* for them. I was on the phone when Guruji walked into the living room. Coming over to me, He told me to open my hand and then manifested the holy ash directly into it. He went to another devotee, who was also in the room, gave some *vibhuti* to her and then proceeded to pour the rest over the flowers which were on the table.

I swallowed the whole heap of *vibhuti* at once and felt so energised that I couldn't sleep that entire night.

*****

On one occasion, I had the opportunity to be next to Guruji when He was giving short interviews to guests. Some people asked questions, others brought items for blessing, and one person brought a photo of his sick girlfriend.

Guruji held the photo in His hands. When the person was leaving, He looked up and made some gestures with the index finger of His right hand. I remembered seeing Him make similar gestures in the past.

When the interviews ended, I asked Guruji what He was doing with His hand. Though not very pleased with my question, He answered, 'Let's say... I can change things.'

*****

One evening I approached Guruji with a question and at the end of our conversation I told Him that He had a beautiful fragrance. He explained that from different parts of his body, different fragrances would manifest. He rubbed a bit on His arm and asked me to smell, it was the fragrance of rose, and then He rubbed on His neck, it was the fragrance of frankincense.

Worldwide, Guruji's devotees experience His divine fragrance, not only when He is physically present, but also when He is far away.

*****

One morning I woke up and found, on my bed and the area surrounding it, small golden-coloured particles. I got out of bed, wondering where this gold dust could have come from. At that time, the hinges on my door squeaked whenever the door moved, making it impossible for anyone to enter without me noticing.

After pondering the situation for a couple of moments, the only explanation I could come up with was, it was another wonder. I suddenly remembered that some time before, I had bowed down in front of my altar and, upon rising, saw these same particles at the place where my head had touched the ground. At that time, I figured it was just mere dust and so threw it away. This second time, however, I carefully collected the particles and they have been kept on my altar ever since.

* * * * *

There was a devotee and her small daughter who lived upstairs, just above my room. Guruji had given them a beautiful, wooden Madonna. The statue constantly poured out holy oil.

* * * * *

Before waking up one morning, I was aware of a pleasing presence around me. Someone was there, fixing something in my subtle body which felt like some type of energetic intervention. I couldn't see anything but was fully aware of the whole process. When I woke up, I was able to feel it throughout my physical body as well.

That afternoon I met Guruji and told Him about this incident. He said that we are sometimes visited and supported by healer saints. 'It was Saint Pantaleimon and his friends', he explained. As it turned out, they came and helped me several more times.

* * * * *

Guruji often told us that Divine Beings and saints would visit Him. Some were physically visible, disguised in a most uncommon way, so that we wouldn't recognise them. At other times, we would observe Guruji being completely lost in some other dimension. Later, He would reveal that a certain Divinity had been there to commune with Him.

They would frequently visit Guruji and often leave Him with a message and a blessing for everyone.

# The Mind

Generally, I struggled with the inability to control my mind and keep it positive. There was a deep-rooted impression that God or *guru* didn't love and care for me.

The more I wished to connect with Guruji from the outside, the more He showed me that this was not the way. He told me that I should come into my own power and find Him inside of my heart.

Prior to living in the *ashram*, it was my regular practice to meditate and connect with Him from inside. Being in His physical proximity, however, I now wanted to have a nice relationship with Him on the outside too. What added to my struggle was that His behaviour confused me at times. He was so Divine, but He seemed to be very human too.

When I addressed this topic with Him once, He said, 'Nobody can understand me. I am a teacher like none before. I teach differently. Only I can understand myself.'

He continued, 'Among the humans, I am the most human. Among the Divine, I am the most Divine. Don't try to understand me. Even Babaji can't understand me. I am beyond understanding!'

He then added, 'I am a good actor. I know everything that is going on in everyone, but I play. I have to play. And when my work is done, I will go.'

His eyes were fixed at some unknown point when He concluded, 'From silence I come. In silence I go.'

When I asked Him why He was ignoring me, he explained, 'I need to do it, to play those roles. I am not doing it because I want to, but because *you* have to learn something and to become strong.' Looking at me, He said, 'I am your mirror, showing what is inside of you and what you still need to work on. I challenge the mind, so that one can cross over its limitations.'

I felt that He was addressing my pride and arrogance, which is so often an obstacle on the spiritual path, by showing me that it needed to be humbled and transformed.

To this end, I went through very deep processes. On certain days, I felt some heaviness which blurred my intellect and vision. I often felt weak, I developed a terrible cough and I had tremendous tension in my body. It was like something invisible was pressing on me and I couldn't breathe. A few times, I suspected that I might have some serious illness, but Guruji explained that these symptoms were coming from the (negative) mind and were draining my energy and weakening me. He advised me not to focus on it, saying, 'Ignore it, don't strengthen it with your thoughts.' He also gave me some additional breathing exercises for controlling the breath.

Guruji emphasised that the mind needs to be controlled and transformed, but the more I analysed the mind and tried to find some solution, the more I got entangled in it. When I asked Him if He knew how difficult transforming the mind was, He answered, 'Yes, I know. Not only for you, but for the whole world and that's why I am here.'

He went on to explain that *bhakti* was not possible without the 'churning of the ocean', that the purification process needs to happen, and it requires time. He advised me not to fight the mind. Instead, I needed to accept and ignore it, to say 'no' to the negative thoughts, replace them with positive ones, and to see myself in other people.

During a meeting, Guruji encouraged me not to give up, saying, 'All of you here are great souls. Many, many would like to be here, but only a few can be. I chose those who won't take long.' He added, 'Open yourself more, it's not necessary anymore for you to live in a cave.'

Since I was often secluded, I wondered if He meant in the here and now, or if He was talking about some past life, and so I tried to clarify: 'Do you mean a real cave or an inner cave?'

'Well, it's the same,' was His reply.

'Why did I incarnate?', I asked.

He explained, 'I will tell you the story of Lahiri Mahasaya. Lahiri was a great *yogi* from the Himalayas, who had a wish to have a golden palace. Therefore, he came back to earth to experience it, but in everything he did in his life, he was with God.'

'Why have I separated myself from God? I want to go home,' I said.

He answered, 'You will! You separated yourself because of the experience and there was still something to be dissolved. You are here to give.' Later, he added in a soft voice, 'Soon the light will shine through you.'

Hearing this from the Master was truly a saving grace, and I wanted to ensure the date, 'Soon? I really hope that it won't take long anymore.' He just reminded me, 'Don't confuse yourself with the time. Don't have any expectations.'

Guruji explained that my name stands for the three eyed Divine Mother (the third being the spiritual eye) and ever since then, I started to like my name. He also told me to see difficult situations as a test, a lesson to be learned. I should not expect things, but to rather take them as they come. 'It is about faith and becoming unshakable in whatever comes on your path. Surrender more and give everything to the feet of God and *guru*.'

He clarified, 'I am not against you, I am against your mind.' I was not aware enough at that time to distinguish between myself and the mind.

Once I asked Him, 'When we don't feel love inside of us, how do we reconnect with it?'

He answered, 'By knowing that love is always there; that you are love. It doesn't depend on anything but is merely covered over because you go through certain things in life.'

When I described to Him that I could feel neither an inner nor an outer connection with Him, Guruji explained that, 'It is because you do not have the inner connection. This is also why you perceive me as not noticing you. The connection with me is always there, but your feelings, the *maya* covers it. The mind needs to be calm.'

During these times of struggle, I would occasionally remember what a grace it was to have Guruji in my life and recognise His boundless mercy and sacrifice for us. A deep feeling of love and thankfulness would arise within me, and I would calm down and find inner peace. The mind, however, would start harassing me again and, after a while, I would approach Guruji once again.

One time He told me, 'I could stop your mind instantly, but what would you learn from it? What would you say, when someone asks you later on, "How did you manage it?" Will you say, "Guruji did it for me?"' He added, 'You need to learn from it.

The path is important so that later you can help other people.'

Even though it was obvious that Guruji did everything to help me, I was not willing or able to surrender. A part of me still wanted to be independent.

After an intense event, I would feel hypersensitive, tired and would stay in bed, not wanting to see anyone. Sometimes, I would take the car and drive somewhere just to be alone. Guruji mentioned to me, 'People run away instead of facing things and dissolving them. To where would you run away from God, from the Essence? Everywhere you go, It will be with you.' And He stressed, 'Don't pity yourself. Don't go into your weakness, go into your strength. It's time to change!'

With time, it became evident that my behaviour and my rebellious attitude were immature. There was something wild inside of me which needed to be tamed, and I wished to improve and be more useful for Him and His mission.

*****

One of my greatest fears was that I would allow my mind to convince me to leave the *ashram*, or even worse, to leave the *guru*. I was aware that the mind can be the best friend when controlled, and the worst enemy when uncontrolled, as Krishna stated in the *Bhagavad Gita*.

One night I dreamt about an earthquake and a voice announcing something about leaving Him. I was left feeling worried and, at the earliest opportunity, approached Guruji and told Him about it. To my surprise, He said, 'I know about it, but you will not leave.'

I looked at Him and replied, 'Guruji, you know, but I don't know.'

'Don't worry', He said, giving me a fatherly embrace. 'You will leave when I tell you to leave.'

Guruji often reminded me not to worry, and that many things I perceived were simply due to fear. When I asked Guruji why I have those dreams and visions and if they were true or illusory, He said, 'It's not illusion but don't hang onto them. Go further. They are showing the path, but there is something greater beyond them.'

Once, I had a dream about a man whom, at one time, I had liked very much. It was about our connection from the past, which awoke some special feelings in me. I spoke with Guruji about it. He asked me straight away, 'Do you want to be with him?'

'Not physically', I replied, 'But if our souls...'

'Forget it!' Guruji interrupted me. 'You have paid already. Or do you want to create new *karma*?'

'Is our connection *karmic*?' I asked.

'Yes.' Guruji replied, 'And you have paid. Therefore, I have accepted you as *brahmacharini.*' He concluded, 'People dream about their imaginations. Do you see how the mind can lead one astray?'

I immediately understood what He was telling me and didn't allow myself to fall into such an illusion anymore.

Another time when I told Him that I would like to find my Divine husband, He answered, 'You will find Him inside. He is part of you'.

When I told Guruji, about hearing His voice inside of me, He clarified: 'It's still not clear, be still and calm, as the imagination of yours is still strong.'

I slowly started realising why Guruji emphasised that without a *satguru* it was impossible to cross over the ocean of *samsara* and attain the final destination. The delusion was luring at every corner; what at first appears to be a nectar, would soon turn into a poison. The *samskaras* (old impressions from the past) would wait to take over when we least expect it. But all of these would only be visible to His eyes, since our eyes were still blinded by the desires and *karma*.

The only way was to hold firmly to Guruji's hand and not let go.

# The Path

After moving to the *ashram*, I asked myself how long I would stay there and what was the purpose of my stay. Guruji would often give hints without saying anything openly. He once told me that later I would be spreading *bhakti*. Since I couldn't imagine what or where this could be, I asked if it would be in Serbia or somewhere else.

'What would you do in Serbia?', he commented, and thus I understood, it wouldn't be there.

Another time, after having some dream about America, I wondered if Guruji would send me there one day. When I asked Him about it, with a slight shake of His head He answered, 'No, I won't live in America.' I looked at Him and was about to say, 'Guruji, I didn't ask about you,' but in the same moment I understood His sweet message: I will be wherever His presence is.

One night I became aware that I was inwardly repeating a long, complex Shiva *mantra* which was completely unknown to me. I perceived myself as being in between Shivaloka, which was somewhere underneath me, and Krishna's abode which was above me. By repeating this *mantra* I was slowly falling downwards towards Shivaloka when I heard myself crying out, 'No, I want to go to Krishna!", and began to call His name and chant *om namo narayanaya.*

When I asked myself why I had to go through such difficult times, the answer came through the following dream: I saw myself from the past, as someone who had a powerful position. Once, when a certain message reached me, I got furious and acted out of madness. My rage apparently led to the death of someone who was innocent. Some 'helpers' restrained me, bandaged my whole body, and carried me out of the scene. I then saw myself, at a later time, in solitude for rehabilitation. I was in a calm state and most of the wounds on my body were already healed. The bandages from my body were almost all removed. However, my head and eyes were still covered, preventing me from seeing. With patience and endurance, I awaited my full recovery.

*****

At times, I would again face some state of distress in Guruji's presence, which almost always happened spontaneously. On one side He was so close to me, and on the other, He could feel so far away. In my heart, I wished to fall at His Feet and surrender, but the mind held me back; feelings of guilt and unworthiness mixed with the impression that He wouldn't care about me.

In addition, as mentioned earlier, I was experiencing very intense pressures inside of myself that could only be described as some type of invisible strings or bundles enveloping my subtle body. The pressure was gradually moving up towards my chest area, thereby affecting and reducing my breathing capacity. The more agitated I was, the stronger the pressure became. However, with the practice of Atma Kriya Level Two, the layers started dissolving much faster. Guruji said, 'It's the old pain from the past. Don't go into it.'

During a Holi celebration in the *ashram*, Guruji was in a very playful state and was throwing colours on those of us in attendance. After exhausting His stock of colours, He continued the festivities by throwing flour. It became a wild, white-coloured Holi, with the residents joyfully throwing flour on one another.

I quietly observed all of this joyful playing as I stood at a distance, incapable of participating. While the others were freely enjoying the party, jumping around and laughing with Guruji, I remained separated, not daring to go any closer. Finally, not able to hold myself back any longer, I ran to a lonely corner and wept bitterly. I didn't know the reason for these feelings or actions, but at that moment, crying by myself was the only relief I could find. After some time, I composed myself and went back. When the party finished, I took the courage to approach Guruji, asking,

'Why do I have such feelings towards you?'

He only said, 'You will know why.'

During another interview with Him, I asked again, 'Why this feeling of guilt? What have I done?'

'I am not allowed to show you, as you are not strong enough yet', He replied. 'From the human point of view, there is good and bad. From the Divine sight, there is only good because everything has its reason. When you can see things positively, when you are ready, it will be shown to you. Patience.' He concluded, 'You will get better, it's just a period. You will receive help and get over it.'

From then on, it was clear there was something which I was not being allowed to remember.

* * * * *

Approximately one year after moving to the *ashram*, my mother invited the closest members of the family for a joint holiday in Cuba. It was a well-organised, two-week tour through the whole country. For me, the trip was an opportunity to say goodbye to my family, as it seemed that we would not see each other often in the next years. I asked Guruji about going and He gave His permission.

The tour was nice; the family was together, and we visited beautiful places throughout the island. However, I felt out of place. Not only was this holiday of no use for my spiritual growth, but it also did not, in any way, contribute to the welfare of the world. It was the essence of the material life which I sought to leave behind.

When I came back to Germany, it was evident that Guruji wasn't pleased with me. In the evening we met in the kitchen, and He said, 'You are a *brahmacharini* and made a commitment. How do you think to go on? To take holidays? Did you enjoy Cuba?'

I felt sorry that he had to remind me about my vows and replied, 'No Guruji, I didn't enjoy it. I know that inside of me something else is waiting.'

He seemed to accept my answer and asked me to sit with Him at the table.

I started a different conversation, 'When I call you in my dreams you are not coming.'

'Even if I would come', he said, 'You would perhaps not recognise me. I am not what people think me to be in this form (body). Only a few know who I am.'

I was listening carefully, while He pointed out, 'What you see of me is only one hundredth of a percent of who I really am.'

I tried to understand His words and asked, 'Guruji, where, then, is the rest of you?'

'I am fully in my body', He clarified, 'But I only *show* one hundredth of a percent of who I am.' Emphasising, 'I am everywhere, working all the time, 365 days, 24 hours a day.'

My next question quickly followed, 'How can we connect with the rest of you?'

'Attach to my form, it's easier. My Cosmic Form is only for a few people.' After a pause, He added, 'With time, you will also know who I am.'

Before He sent me to my room, He stressed, 'I am different from other *gurus*. It is very rare that I come on Earth. Don't waste any more time. Focus on God.'

I went back to my room with a strong determination to give my best from then on.

In the time following this conversation, I intensified my Atma Kriya practice, studied the scriptures, and watched plenty of spiritual movies about the *avatars* of God. All these things contributed to creating a better connection and relationship with the Divine.

After reading the *Bhagavad Gita* and the Gospels, I started writing about the similarities of Sri Krishna and Jesus Christ, as Guruji had requested. He had given a profound discourse on Krishna's life during Krishna Janmashtami and compared it with the life of Christ, so I included all of those details in my writing. Additionally, I also included information I gleaned from my research on the Internet. It became a script of 15 pages, including many pictures.

When the day came to present the writing to Guruji, all the *matajis* who were asked to prepare something, gathered in the living room. When I arrived, He was already sitting at the table going through the scripts, one by one. Some of them He read for a while and some He threw aside after a few seconds commenting how useless they were. When He took mine, I was trembling and wished to disappear. To my amazement, He spent the longest time on it. After reading it for a while He paused and commented,

'Huhhh, she read, *The Second Coming of Christ*.'

I quickly tried to remember if this was some part of the *Bible* or something else, and it flashed into my mind that it was a book written by Paramahansa Yogananda. Straight away, I explained myself, 'No, I didn't read it.'

Guruji was still scanning the pages and repeated, 'Yes, you read it.'

One of the *matajis* jokingly concluded, 'Maybe she read the book in her past life!'

I didn't dare say anything and remained silent, waiting for Guruji's final feedback.

He gave me the script back with the words, 'It's a good direction but go more deeply into it.'

In the following years, I gradually worked on it and, by His grace, it eventually became a book.

As Guruji started initiating people into Atma Kriya Yoga, all the courses in the *ashram* were fully booked. My additional *seva* became organising and coordinating the courses and scheduling.

He appointed several *Kriya Yoga* teachers for these courses, and I was one of them. My first course was in Belgrade in 2008, during a Darshan tour through Serbia and Croatia. I was teaching the students, and Guruji gave the Shaktipat.

In general, I was insecure and uncomfortable with public speaking. Only by His blessing and through His encouraging words, 'Go for it!', was I able to gradually develop self-confidence and teach freely.

By knowing the potential and the *dharma* of every person, and how to develop it, Guruji would engage someone with the duties, where one's best qualities would unfold, naturally leading to a wider perspective. What would appear as some coincidence from the outside, would have a deeper meaning and an agenda behind it, known only to Guruji.

# His Care for the Family

Throughout the years, I could observe, that the Master doesn't only elevate His devotees, but He also cares for their families.

In the beginning of our spiritual path, the family might feel neglected or consider us egoistic. The truth is, that our focus changes and turns from our egoistic self towards our true Self, the *atma*. This is the place where we are all connected on the inside and relate to each other from the space of unconditional love. The more we are in tune with our soul, the more the family, and everyone around us, benefits from it.

Our parents, especially, might think they know what is best for us. Their love, however, is often limited due to attachment and personal expectations. A *satguru*, on the contrary, is free of any attachment or selfish motive. He knows our soul and oversees and guides our whole evolutionary process. Hence, He truly knows what is best for us and how to help us reach the goal of life in the quickest way.

There was a period where I was sad about my disharmonious childhood. In my younger years, I dearly liked to spend time with my father, but, later due to his unstable character, I learnt to keep my distance. From puberty on, I started opposing him, usually standing up for my mother. It was only after my own marriage that our relationship improved, leaving behind some void space. The old wounds and the unspoken words were still standing between us.

One day, I rebelled inside myself, wondering why it had to be the way it had been and why I couldn't have enjoyed my childhood in a harmonious family, with a gentle and understanding father. The next morning, before waking up, the following insight came: 'Be glad, that it was not easy. If it would have been, you wouldn't have developed to reach where you are now. You wouldn't have searched for the path, for God. In lives, where you had a gentle father, you didn't learn much. You think only about yourself, but now you can serve!'

After this message, my view on things started to change, and I began to see my family as souls, who were given to me on my life journey. I started looking for opportunities to support them on their spiritual path.

* * * * *

Shortly after I had moved to the *ashram*, my ex-husband came for an interview with Guruji. Our life paths had separated after I had met my *satguru*, and it was still difficult for him to open himself up to a new relationship.

When he entered the interview room, he was extremely nervous and couldn't speak until Guruji placed His fingers on his temple, which calmed him down. He was very open towards Guruji, expressing that he would like to have a family and find his path in life. It was apparent that Guruji invisibly embraced his whole being, saying, 'Don't worry. You will have both.' He then materialised a beautiful pendant, with a Sri Yantra on one side and Maha-Lakshmi on the other, for him. In a caring way, Guruji further explained to us that our *karma* together had finished. When I made a funny comment, 'We surely must have had several terrible lives together', Guruji just smiled and gave me a confirming gesture.

After a few months, my ex-husband started a new relationship. When he and his new wife eventually had their first child, I informed Guruji about it. He jokingly asked me, 'Are you jealous?'

'I am still jealous, but not towards him', was my answer, whereupon Guruji just laughed.

*****

My mother met Guruji when she and I came together for our first interview and she considered Him as someone very dear, wise and miraculous.

She was not a follower but while she was still living in Germany, she visited us regularly.

When my parents divorced, my father remarried, and my mother entered another complicated relationship. It went so far that she developed some serious problems and health issues. I advised her to come to the *ashram* more often, and since she liked baking, she would also bring something for Guruji to eat. He addressed her several times as 'Mamma'.

On one day Guruji called my mother for an interview in the church. While she was narrating her story, Guruji was sitting next to her looking slightly up, as though observing something. Regardless of what my mother was saying, He already knew what her soul needed. He gave her some advice and materialised a small *rudraksha* bead that was to be worn around her neck.

Very shortly after this meeting, my mother's health stabilised, her partner simply left, and another man came into her life. She got an early retirement and they both went back to Serbia, living harmoniously together, until the present day.

* * * * *

My father, on the contrary, was against my path and Guruji from the very beginning. He couldn't accept the fact that I left the 'comfortable' material life and a 'promising future' for the sake of 'some preacher'. The material reality was everything and all he wanted to know, and despite our many conversations and discussions, he would not change his mind.

One afternoon he and his wife visited me in the *ashram*. Guruji was about to leave for America but spontaneously gave a Darshan on that day. Since they were there, I invited them to stay and take the blessing from Guruji. My father's wife agreed to it, and together, we both convinced my father to stay as well. After all, it was a chance for him to see and experience Guruji from another perspective. He had met Him a few times, but each time remained critical towards Him.

After Guruji arrived and the Darshan started, I called them to line up together. My father hesitated again, but eventually came. On the way to Guruji, I informed them not to be surprised if they feel anxiety or a strong heartbeat in His proximity. My father just rolled his eyes, energetically saying that he 'doesn't believe in these things'.

First his wife received Darshan, and then my father and me. We were kneeling in front of Guruji at the same time, but my father received the blessing before I did. As Darshan is an intimate moment, I looked down. However, when I noticed my father shaking, I looked over at him. While he was receiving the blessing, he was crying like a child. I could not believe my eyes. It was like a dream. Only once in my life had I ever seen my father crying.

After I received the blessing, I told Guruji that this was my father. 'The man who cried?' He asked. 'He is a nice man.' When I heard this, I couldn't help but smile.

I was happy for my father. Happy that he had finally found a deeper connection with himself. His beautiful essence had tried for years to express itself but his mind would not allow it. As he was overwhelmed with the experience, maybe even somewhat embarrassed, he left with his wife shortly after. Two weeks later we met again, but to my regret, his old impressions had again taken over. His mind spoke louder than his heart and he didn't want to hear anything about Guruji.

Sometime after, Guruji asked about him and I disclosed, 'He still thinks that I have missed the point of life.'

'You should ask him first, if he has found and fulfilled his own purpose in life!' was Guruji's answer. Later his advice became, 'Just pray for him.'

* * * * *

In the early *ashram* years, when my sister and her family came for a visit, I had a strong wish that Guruji would materialise something for my nieces as a protection for them.

Guruji was there on that day and called the whole family for an interview in the temple. My two nieces received earrings from Guruji. Even though He didn't do it in front of their eyes, I knew that they were materialised gifts. My eldest niece was not there, and I reminded Guruji about her. 'Ah, yes', He said, and with His hand placed underneath His shawl, He manifested a beautiful silver ring with a yellow-crystal star for her.

We all felt very blessed, and my sister and her husband became more open to some new ideas. We could speak about spirituality, something which in the past was not a possible topic of conversation between us. However, this state of openness didn't last long, as they couldn't follow up with this experience.

My eldest niece wore the ring throughout her youth and felt very protected, until one day it disappeared. I told her not to worry, as the ring had fulfilled its purpose.

* * * * *

At some point, I felt a strong pull to give Atma Kriya Yoga initiation to my family. My grandpa, a humble and goodhearted person who took care of me when I was small, was already very old. I knew that the power of Shaktipat itself would benefit him in his after- or next life. Guruji agreed to it, and I went to Serbia to organise the course with my mother, sister, grandpa, cousin and a friend.

Even though my family was not familiar with this kind of spirituality, they carefully listened, followed the exercises, and were appreciating the course. Grandpa couldn't do all the practices, but he was the best at OM Chanting, since he used to be a singer in his youth. With a high, strong OM, he made us all laugh.

He passed away a year after the initiation.

*****

Once, when there was a problem in my family, I asked Guruji what I should do with regards to it. 'You are dead for the world and especially for your family,' He answered.

Though it may sound harsh or difficult to accept, for me, it was a blessing to be reminded by Him not to get entangled into worldly drama and to keep my focus on God. This was also the best way to support my family.

Next to our individual *karma*, there is our family *karma*. We incarnate together with our family members for a reason, to learn and to then complete something. By neutralising our own *karma* through the *sadhana* and by the grace of the *guru*, the collective *karma* is being transformed and our families benefit from it too.

Ultimately, if an individual frees him- or herself by His grace, they naturally become a lighthouse and a blessing for everyone around them. Not only for those in their immediate proximity, but for many generations before and after this particular life.

# The New Ashram

An increasing number of people started to learn about, and follow, Guruji.

In the meantime, He received the title '*Paramahamsa*', the 'Great Swan', by Mahavatar Babaji. It describes the state beyond the influences of material nature and ability to separate the real from the unreal, the spiritual from material.

In 2008 Guruji initiated His first *swamis* as main representatives of Bhakti Marga who would support His mission in the world.

As Guruji travelled to different countries throughout the world – Poland, Portugal, England, Russia, Croatia, Italy, South Africa, Kenya, America, and wherever else He would go – a good number of devotees would follow. Thus, the visitors in the *ashram* increased day by day, until it was clear that we needed a bigger space.

A team of devotees was formed to begin searching for other premises to become the home of a new, larger Bhakti Marga *ashram*. At the end of 2007, the project team found a suitable building complex, only an hour's drive from Steffenshof. It was situated in the beautiful countryside of Heidenrod, on a hill at the edge of Springen village. Due to the fact that the complex had been abandoned for several years, the purchase price wasn't much, but the expected restoration expenses were huge.

The *prabhus* moved to the property first in order to begin making the main building functional. After a few months, the *matajis* followed, contributing to the general cleaning and cooking, as well as, organising and carrying out various community affairs.

In the beginning, the *prabhus* were accommodated in the village but eventually moved into the *ashram*. Everyone chose a room in the main building, *matajis* and *prabhus* on different floors, while Guruji moved into one of the modest cottages on the property. Soon a small temple was installed, and the prayers could continue.

The first years in Springen were marked with uncertainty. It was a transition time, a period where many devotees left Guruji, and no one knew what direction Bhakti Marga would move in or how it would develop.

The focus was on renovations and making the main building functional for public access. The installation of fire-protection equipment was required, and the rooms had to be renovated and furnished. In addition, the heating was not functioning properly, which gave us the opportunity for an austere life. As there were only 25 residents at the time, Bhakti Marga didn't have enough finances or *seva* workers. Hence the renovations were done gradually.

2010 was a critical time for Bhakti Marga. Guruji asked His devotees to support with the renovation and opening process of the *ashram*. He explained that the *ashram* was not for Himself but was to become a spiritual fountain and shelter for all of the current devotees, as well as, all those to come in the future. In closer circles, He explained that our *ashram*, with all the prayers and spiritual practices that we did and would do, would nourish the surrounding area and, on a higher plane, would benefit the whole world. The generated spiritual vibration released into the world would transform and elevate the consciousness of people and essentially contribute to dissolving the cause of misery. The support of the devotees increased in the following years, and the renovation work steadily progressed. Guruji named our *ashram*, 'Shree Peetha Nilaya', the Abode of the Divine Mother, Maha-Lakshmi.

As we started organising regular public events, we noticed that the same people would participate again and again. We knew every person, and only once in a while was there a new guest in the *ashram*. After some time, Guruji told us that He would like to see new faces.

He continued travelling and giving Darshan all over the world, while we (the devotees in the *ashram*) put forth an increasing effort to spread His teachings to new people in new areas. At this time, I was put in charge of OM Chanting and Guruji told me to support the spread of Bhakti Kriya, which in 2008 He renamed Atma Kriya, stating that 'people are still not ready for *bhakti*'.

In the beginning, Guruji was the only one giving Shaktipat to the kriya students. At some point, He told us to pray that Mahavatar Babaji would allow teachers to give Shaktipat too. When this happened near the end of 2008, Guruji empowered around twenty teachers to give Shaktipat initiation for Atma Kriya Level One. I was one of them.

During the three last days of the teacher course, we did a purification ritual where we were to call upon our *ishtadeva* (worshipper's favourite deity from all lives). For this, Guruji told us to choose the Divinity we feel most close to. I was not sure if it was Mother Mary or Christ, but Guruji helped me with the decision, by saying, 'Mother Mary is also in Him', and so I chose Christ as my *ishtadeva*.

Before initiating us, Guruji called us to Him, one by one. He asked us three questions and in order to pass the test, at least two of them had to be answered correctly. When it was my turn, Guruji, with a firm, deep voice, asked,

'Triambhakeshwari, why do you want to teach Atma Kriya?'

I was already nervous, but after hearing His voice, it was like Babaji Himself was questioning me. In time, I answered, 'To bring more love and light to the world, and to fulfil my task.'

'Serving, would be the right answer', He said, 'It's nothing about fulfilling your task.'

'Why are you practising Atma Kriya?' was His next question.

'To come back home, to go back to God,' I replied.

'You don't know who God is', He commented, 'Love is the right answer.'

Becoming aware that it was the second question incorrectly answered, I objected, 'But God is Love.'

'God is more than Love. God is everything', He corrected me and asked the third question:

'Who is your Gurudev?'

With great confidence I answered, 'You!'

'Well,' He said, 'You have answered two questions wrong and one right.' After a short pause He concluded, 'But you have passed.'

I felt humiliated, and responded, 'If I am not ready for it, I don't need to do it.'

Softening His tone, He replied, 'No, you have passed. You can do it.'

Guruji was an expert in keeping our pride down, and at the same time giving us all the support and blessings to move upwards, towards our *dharma*. The entire teacher course, along with the initiation, was yet another elevating event after which, I could feel Guruji more present inside of me.

Sometime later, during a nap, I had an interesting, clear dream. Viewing a world map, I watched myself moving like a wind from the Balkans area over Turkey and Greece towards the Middle East. At the same time, an audible voice was prophesying that I would spread *bhakti* in those areas. I woke up wondering how this would ever be possible.

With time, I started travelling to different countries giving OM Chanting workshops, Atma Kriya Yoga and Mudra courses. The trajectory I was following naturally led me toward the Balkan countries, and from there further and further towards the Middle East...

# The Nun

In 2012, I was travelling by car throughout the Balkans spreading OM Chanting and Atma Kriya Yoga. Throughout my travels, I visited several beautiful monasteries and enjoyed the late spring nature.

First, I went to Serbia and from there to Bulgaria. In Sofia, we organised several OM Chanting sessions and the Bulgarians connected me further to a friend in Macedonia, where I travelled next.

There, I was warmly welcomed by a lady who needed a few days to prepare for our OM Chanting event at her studio. She offered for me to stay at her home, but I preferred to go to a monastery. She recommended I stay at a certain monastery not far away from the capital.

I drove there, and found a beautiful convent, situated on a hill near a river surrounded by untouched nature. It had an ancient and richly painted church from the 14th century, a convent and a guest house. It was a serene place with only a few nuns living there. I met the mother of the convent and asked her if it was possible to stay there for three days.

'Do you have the blessing?' she asked.

I smiled, since I was thinking to myself, 'I have many blessings: blessings for organising OM Chanting, for Atma Kriya Yoga initiation, and so on', and eventually answered, 'Yes, I do from my spiritual father.'

She messaged *her* spiritual father to approve and, when he also agreed, they welcomed me, brought some food and showed me to my accommodations.

The guest house was a beautiful old building with oriental belvederes. Since the 16th century, the monastery had operated uninterrupted, and you could feel the strong monastic spirit and deep calm that pervaded the grounds.

While sitting on the belvedere with a beautiful view to the ancient church, I used this time to continue writing on the similarities between Hinduism and Christianity. From time to time, the mother would come with a small, Turkish coffee and we would sit together, conversing nicely.

She asked me what I was doing, but I felt that I couldn't tell her since she might not tolerate it. However, when I mentioned *yoga* to her, she remained open-minded, saying that she knew some people who practised Hinduism. Unlike other clergy members I had experiences with, she was not judgmental of other religions. Little by little, I started sharing with her about Guruji, our spiritual father, and the *ashram*.

In the evening, I joined the residents for their prayers under the candlelight. The melodious hymns and the Jesus prayer touched me deeply and evoked in me a profound longing. I missed the traditional monastic life; to wear a habit, to be in a contemplative mood, and to have a serene inner connection with the Lord.

In the new *ashram*, we were always busy and in a hurry. We didn't wear a uniform at that time, even if Guruji encouraged us to do so, and since we had many visitors coming, they didn't necessarily recognise us as *brahmacharis*. Often, they would want to chat and hug us. Some even showed romantic interest in the residents. Moreover, many short-term residents were coming, bringing with them all different kinds of interests and intentions. As a result, the overall *ashram* atmosphere was slowly changing into a modern spiritual centre.

My whole experience in the monastery left a deep impression on me. Since we also had a church back home at the *ashram*, I started to consider asking Guruji to bless me for Christian monasticism.

The OM Chanting event in Macedonia was amazing and I felt that I had found some new members of our bigger Bhakti Marga family. I went from there to Albania and further on to Montenegro.

Due to a long drive, I became very tired in Albania. My body was burning from the inside, and I eventually had to stop on the roadside to take a nap in the car.

During that nap, I had a short dream where a girl said, 'You were not good in a few lives (referring to the inner burning and tension I had been feeling). It will go away with the third initiation.' I woke up and had to face, again, some unknown past and assumed that the third initiation was the third level of Atma Kriya Yoga.

With Guruji's blessing, the journey continued through several other Balkan countries, leaving behind a seed which, I trusted, would germinate in due time.

*****

The same year I went with a group of Atma Kriya *yogis* to the Himalayas, where we visited many holy places and areas connected with Mahavatar Babaji.

On that trip, I received several inner revelations. One night I dreamt about how busy I used to be with finding and buying nice clothes that fit me well. This had, indeed, been a preoccupation in my youth. I also remember being told in the dream that, 'This is not necessary anymore. Soon, you will have the clothes of your life.'

When I returned from that trip, I asked Guruji if He would give me the blessing to become a Christian nun.

'Why do you want it?' He asked, 'You are already a brahmacharini.' After a pause, He added, 'Let's see after Navaratri', which is one of the most revered Hindu festivals observed for the Divine Mother.

In the meantime, I had another interesting dream with Saint Benedict. I recognised him from the icon in our church but then he gradually changed into Guruji. He told me, 'You could start an order. I trust you and will support you.'

At my earliest opportunity, I informed Guruji about it. He reluctantly responded, 'What will be in the future, will be.'

After some time, I sent Guruji a letter asking Him, 'if becoming a nun is beneficial for me, help me to fulfil it, and if not, help me to forget it.'

When we met a week later, upon His return from Greece, He gave me the blessing with the instruction to wear black robes from then onwards.

I was grateful that Guruji allowed me to take this step and was busy adapting into the new lifestyle and learning more about Christianity and Orthodoxy. Some people in the *ashram* were supportive of such an opportunity within Bhakti Marga and others were critical.

I contacted the mother from Macedonia and told her the good news. She was happy for me but, at the same time, she couldn't really comprehend our version of Christianity. The biggest difference in the discussions between us concerned the belief of reincarnation. The Christian faith teaches that there is only one life after which one either goes to an eternal heaven or hell.

Guruji said that in Early Christianity, the belief in reincarnation existed. However, it was removed during one of the Ecumenical Councils. One of the reasons was to give the leadership better control over the people and to make them strive, out of fear, for salvation during one lifetime.

The existence of reincarnation is very logical and becomes increasingly evident through the personal experiences of many people, especially children, who are born with the gift to see or to remember their past lives. This understanding was something that I really missed within Christianity and I consider it an essential element (of the Cosmic Law) to understand life and life circumstances. Without *karmic* law, God would appear unjust, giving different living conditions to people at random.

Despite our differences around this topic, the mother gave me a lot of useful advice in connection with monasticism and Orthodoxy and, over time, we became good friends. I admired her compassionate heart, her faith and deep dedication.

Shortly after me, another *brahmacharini* expressed her desire to become a nun. Guruji gave her some time to prepare herself and she became a nun six months after me.

I had several dreams of *brahmacharinis* who could also potentially become nuns. Once, when I met Guruji, He asked me who I thought could become the next nun. I mentioned the person from the dream, saying, 'I think she would be a good nun.'

'Yes,' was His confirmation.

When I commented, 'But, it is on her to realise it,', He jokingly replied, 'But you can put some fuel into it.'

I told her about it, and shortly after, she decided to ask Guruji about becoming a nun. Soon, we were three nuns and Guruji made it clear that He wanted me to be the abbess.

He told us that Bhakti Marga purchased a house in the village which would soon become a convent for us. The living room would be reconstructed into a church and for that we received a beautiful project to prepare the iconostasis together with a team of Bhakti Marga artists.

We moved into the house at the end of 2013 and started transforming it into a convent.

# The Convent

Guruji didn't give us a specific agenda for the convent. He wanted us to have community prayers and a sisterhood but left it up to us to plan and organise our community life. He advised us not to take on the traditional way of monasticism, as this would not even be possible within Bhakti Marga. We were still active in His mission and continued our *seva* in the *ashram*.

The painting of the iconostasis, which was done predominantly in white and gold colours, progressed well. According to Guruji's instructions, Christ, Mary, and all the saints had a white robe with a golden background which gave them a majestic appearance.

For the Sanctuary, we painted a Holy Trinity icon: Christ as Father, Son and The Holy Spirit with three faces and six hands in the sign of blessing. The original icon, from which we took our inspiration, is located at Mount Athos in Greece, but our version is even more magnificent.

On April 1, 2015, Guruji officially blessed our church, dedicating it to Mary Magdalene and St. Claude of Besancon. On that same day, He blessed a new nun and made me a mother of the convent.

Guruji gave an inspiring talk, saying that everyone who participated in the preparations of the iconostasis and the church would always benefit from the prayers held at this place. He also explained that, during the ceremony, Christ Himself entered the Holy Trinity icon. From that moment on, His heart (in the middle of the chest, where a small OM is painted) started to pulsate.

What a blessing this was for us! We had Guruji as our Master and, from then on, we also had the Living Christ residing with us in the convent. Thus, our little convent quickly became a precious jewel.

We started off conducting prayers and services in our church for half the week, and for the other half we attended temple prayers in the *ashram*. Once a week, we studied Christianity, learned traditional orthodox songs and, whenever we had time, we painted icons.

Some months later, the fifth and final nun joined the convent.

With His blessing, Guruji gave us everything needed to develop our monastic life together, and I was grateful for this opportunity and His trust. Over time, He also gave us some guidelines: we needed to be back at the convent by 10 o'clock each night, we could not have any visitors (apart from women who were allowed to join the prayers), and we could not participate in certain Bhakti Marga activities.

All who came to visit the convent were deeply touched by its beauty and the immense blessing they experienced while there. Some women would suddenly start crying, feeling much more connected with Christ and Christianity.

Since the nuns could go inside the sanctuary, I decided one day to place my hand on Christ's heart to feel it beating, and indeed, I could immediately feel its soft, steady pulse. It was a sweet experience, which I shared during a meeting with the other sisters. Two of them revealed that they had done the same. One said that she felt the heartbeat but the other nun said she couldn't feel anything. On one occasion, I asked Guruji about it, and He explained that our experience would depend on our connection to Christ.

Guruji visited us occasionally, mostly bringing some 'holy gifts' for us, looking over the church and spending some time with us. He would go through the house, inspecting and indicating what should be improved or changed. Generally, He was content with our efforts, and we had fun with His visits. He instructed us to wear white robes in the *ashram* and black robes when we were travelling.

Guruji sent our sisterhood on a journey to Macedonia where we had a beautiful time with the mother I had met from there. Another wonderful gift came later when, together with Guruji, we visited the Holy Land. This was a time when we were filled with the most beautiful memories of our sisterhood.

*****

In my new role as a mother, I started observing certain behaviours and attitudes among the nuns which I didn't consider beneficial for the monastic life. Some of them would not attend the prayers, or evade their duties, or would childishly chit-chat. When I would address these issues, the individuals would often feel offended, or would defend one other. I increasingly found myself in a position of not knowing how to manage certain situations or how to address problems without overwhelming the sisters and myself. As Guruji was ultimately in charge of our convent, I asked Him for some advice. For each different situation, He advised me accordingly.

As a support for our sisterhood, we initiated weekly meetings which would create a space to organise our community life, to address any concerns or issues we had, and to clean the house together. The nuns were highly creative, and talented, but had strong characters. Our focal point was Guruji and it was that focus that held us together.

My time in the convent was a period of life when I took the opportunity to dive deeper into the life stories of saints, which awakened greater love and admiration for them. I watched many saints movies, especially from the Coptic Church, which Guruji also adored.

My favourites were the desert fathers, the initiators of the monastic life in the Egyptian deserts: Saint Anthony, Saint Paul, Saint Paissios the Great, but also Mary of Egypt, Holy Merthyr Meena, and many, many others. Egypt was also the country where the Holy Family (Mother Mary, Joseph, and Jesus) took refuge for three and a half years.

With time, I could feel that Egypt was calling me! As Bhakti Marga didn't have any activity there, I started planning a trip to Cairo and Alexandria to give an Atma Kriya Yoga course and several OM Chanting workshops.

Guruji warned me in the beginning because of the unstable situation in the country. I wrote to Him, stating that, 'Even if there is one of Your potential devotees waiting for You, it is worth going.'

He answered, 'Go, bless you. May angels protect you.'

And so, it was.

# The Travelling

Guruji had advised me on several occasions to focus on my strength, and so I involved myself passionately in spreading OM Chanting and Atma Kriya Yoga into the world. In moments of service and dedication, it became easier to forget my unsteady mind and the tensions within my body that I struggled with throughout the years.

It was natural for me to travel and to connect with people. Those I met and communicated with often seemed to be inspired by our interactions. I felt guided by Guruji from inside and developed a feeling for those who were ready to meet Him. Sometimes, however, it was sad for me to see that people would miss this unique chance in their life. It seemed that material attachments, desires or pride were preventing them from meeting Him.

For those who took the step and met Guruji, I witnessed their beautiful transformation. Many people come to Guruji as rough stones and, in due course, become beautiful diamonds.

I travelled to Egypt a few times and later to some other Middle Eastern countries. Egypt, however, was my favourite and each time I was there, it felt like home.

During my first visit, I organised an OM Chanting workshop in a *yoga* studio in Cairo where I also introduced the Atma Kriya course scheduled for the following days.

This would be the first time since Turkey that I experienced OM Chanting in a Muslim country, and I was curious how it would go.

Out of respect for their culture, I dressed in a long, white dress.

Around fifteen participants came together, some were covered, some were very modern, but they all were open to hear something new.

When we started with the chanting, a strong OM vibration filled the whole space, and everyone seemed to enjoy it. In the subsequent sharing round, four participants reported that they could hear 'God is most great' throughout the session. For me, this was another beautiful reassurance that the universal sound of OM was pervading all different beliefs and unifying all people. It confirmed what Guruji had said about how the higher beings and saints were supporting and participating in the chanting, as well.

After the event, a lady approached me. She confided that at the beginning of the session, while the invocation *mantra* was chanted, she saw Guruji and Babaji, standing next to her. She recognised them from the pictures, which were set up during the workshop. We started talking and it was just a matter of time before she realised her deeper connection with Guruji.

She took the Atma Kriya Yoga course on the next day and started practising it regularly. We kept in touch, until one day she met Guruji in Israel. Shortly thereafter, she became a devotee, later, an Atma Kriya Yoga teacher herself, and eventually, one of my dear friends.

In Cairo I was hosted by a nice lady, a revolutionist, who took me to various places to organise OM Chanting and for sightseeing. She also helped me hire a driver for visiting several monasteries in the desert.

We would leave early in the morning and drive throughout the day along the sea and through the desert, until we arrived at a remote place where the monastery would emerge in front of us as a beautiful green oasis. The sky, the sunset, the spirit of those places, the ancient churches, the holy relics, the smell of incense and the herbal mixture of *honout*, would naturally bring one into a contemplative and introspective mood.

The monasteries were mostly founded by saints, who, after receiving enlightenment and living by the grace of God, served as teachers and *gurus* for other monastics and people. As a bright light, they would illuminate the whole area, setting an example and giving direction for the generations to come. Even nowadays, such saints exist.

Wherever we went, the residents welcomed us warmly, showing us the holy places, inviting us for a drink or a meal and giving us some gifts. They would tell us the history and how those monasteries survived throughout the centuries and remained active until today, often with more than a hundred monks or nuns. In times of persecutions and barbarian invasions many monastics even gave their lives.

The faith, the dedication and the simplicity of the Coptic monasticism was exemplary. At the end of each day, I would feel such a fulfilment and freedom from visiting those places and being in the company of fellow lovers of Christ.

During this time, I visited the Cairo Convent, a spiritual pearl situated in the middle of Cairo. While there, I met Mother Superior. She welcomed me with such sweetness and innocence that we kept in touch from that time on and eventually became friends.

I had similar experiences in the other countries I travelled to. I offered Bhakti Marga courses, connected with people from *yoga* circles, and visited holy places whenever there was time or opportunity. With time, the first OM Chanting circles were established and Atma Kriya yogis were initiated in those areas.

Guruji, however, was not too happy about the amount of travelling I was doing during this time.

He wanted me to stay in the convent more, but at the same time, He seemed to be pleased with it. We agreed that I would spend more time in the convent and travel every three months. However, it became increasingly difficult for me to handle the situation in the convent and the travelling turned into a kind of respite for me.

* * * * *

Once, I had a Middle East tour starting in Oman. There was a *yoga* studio in Muscat which agreed to host some of our meditation courses. To my regret, right before leaving for my trip, I was informed that they cancelled everything due to a lack of registrations. As my flight was already booked, I contacted a few more *yoga* studios in Oman, trying to find another place for the courses to be held. One of them was an Indian *yoga* teacher who responded positively and invited me for a conversation at her place. I booked a hotel in Muscat for the first two days, and the rest, I left open to 'go with the flow'.

One hour before my departure, we had a celebration in the church. When I went to receive the blessing from Guruji, He expressed His disapproval of my trip to Oman and my frequent travels, in general. Only after I explained that in addition to the convent, I was still in charge of spreading OM Chanting did He soften a little bit.

I departed for this journey with a deep concern in my heart, 'Maybe this time I really went too far? To travel to a strict Muslim country without any agenda or knowing anyone?'

Arriving in Muscat, I rented the smallest car I could and received a brand-new full-size car with an automatic transmission instead. They gave me a short instruction for use, mentioning that going through a red traffic light in their country was punishable with 24 hours in jail and an additional fine. I took the car and left for the hotel in the middle of the night.

On the broad highway I was the only driver. From both sides of the road, large building-complexes were appearing, illuminating the darkness, while I was focusing on the mobile GPS navigation.

I changed the gear lever to a position, as the young man at the airport had explained, but obviously, this was not the right move. Suddenly, with full braking force, the car stopped in the middle of the highway. Fortunately, it was night, and there were no cars behind me. I immediately changed back the transmission and wondered about how irresponsible it was for the young man to give me wrong instructions, which could have cost me my life. Again, I remembered Guruji's disapproval of the trip and an uncertainty overwhelmed me.

I arrived at the hotel early in the morning and, since it was not possible to enter the room at that hour, I walked towards the sea. As I was going along the street, cars started stopping and men asked me outrageously obscene things. When I eventually mentioned the police, the men left. This was clearly not a place for a woman to walk alone.

I walked back to the car and drove to a nearby city to visit a Hindu Krishna temple which I had previously located on the map. This was one of the options to connect with some Indians and possibly organise an OM Chanting event. When I arrived and asked about it, the temple manager explained that the Sultan must approve bigger gatherings and it would take several weeks to get a response. After taking the blessing from Krishna, I left.

Driving along the coastline I passed through the beautiful old city but was not in the mood for sightseeing and so continued driving. I spontaneously changed the lane before passing through the traffic light and I saw the flash of a traffic camera that captured my car! I was positive that the light had not been red, but the flash was visible! In Europe, such a driving manoeuvre was permitted, but apparently not here. I was stunned. Already imagining the message I would write to Guruji from jail, I was able to compose myself instantly and stayed positive. The whole situation was tiring and I went back to the hotel to sleep until the meeting with the Indian *yoga* teacher.

In the evening, I went to the Indian populated city nearby Muscat and met the lady at her home. It was a pleasant encounter, meeting not only a *yoga* teacher, but a devotee with a small temple in her house with a Kanchi Kamakshi deity and pictures of Shirdi Sai Baba. I told her about OM Chanting, Atma Kriya Yoga, Guruji and our *ashram* in Germany. She was impressed and invited me to organise OM Chanting in her *yoga* studio twice a day throughout my stay. How relieved I was to have found an opportunity to do something spiritual in this country!

I left her place feeling joyful and, while driving back to the hotel, changed lanes again and there came the second flash! I couldn't believe it and eventually just had to take it with humour: for the first two days I booked a hotel, and for the last two I would have free accommodation in the jail. However, it was not funny to be alone in this foreign country.

Early in the morning I headed again towards the *yoga* studio and was amazed when I encountered seventy people, mostly Indians. After explaining the OM Chanting technique and introducing Guruji, we had a huge and beautiful OM Chanting. In the subsequent sharing round several participants shared their deep impressions and the whole group showed interest in regular OM Chanting sessions. At the end, I was invited by the core *yoga* team for a joint breakfast where we conversed about Hinduism and spirituality. It was nice talking to Indians living in a diaspora.

In the evening after a *yoga* class, we had another OM Chanting with a large group of children. The next day was with a group of women and later that day, with a group of men. In between, I trained two ladies to conduct and receive the blessing for OM Chanting.

On my last day, I was invited to give a discourse on the *Bhagavad Gita* during the local Diwali celebration. During the evening, the host informed me that she was going to start a charity project in South India the following year and invited me to come for the opening where I could present and organise OM Chanting.

The Indian community in Oman cared nicely for me and I felt as though I had family all over the world. Some of them even checked with the police about the red-light flashes and let me know that there was nothing to worry about!

I sent Guruji photos from the different activities and wrote in short about the experiences. He sent His love to the whole community, adding, 'I was thinking of what we spoke before you left. I still want you to travel spreading what you have been doing already.'

When I read that, I was so comforted and wrote back, 'Gurudev, I was so sad that You were unhappy with me',

He replied, 'I was not unhappy.'

I also informed Him about the invitation for the charity project in South India, seeing it as an opportunity to spread OM Chanting and His teaching in this area. He was glad about it and gave His blessing. With that, I was able to continue my Middle East journey with a feeling of relief.

*****

Once, I travelled to Dubai to organise an OM Chanting workshop and a Maha-Lakshmi Yagna at the place of a devotee and a dear friend. I arrived late in the night, and I took a pink taxi, which was only for female customers. Seeing an Indian lady at the wheel, I enthusiastically shared with her that I have an Indian *guru*. She gave me an unusual reaction and after some time she expressed, 'I don't believe in many gods, especially not in a God like Krishna who had so many wives.'

This was a surprise to hear, and from her further comments I noticed that she was Christian. Based on her statements, it seemed that she was not sufficiently informed about the Vedic Theology, which promotes one absolute Truth or Supreme Being or original cause from which everything and everyone emanates. All living and non-living beings are supported and sustained by Him. All other deities come from Him, and the goal of all life is to serve and worship Him. The variety of gods in Hinduism should be understood as His many aspects and extensions. In addition, there is a variety of demigods or *devas*, which would correlate to the archangels and angels within Christianity.

After her statement about Krishna, I reminded her of the dual nature of Christ, who is believed to be fully divine and fully human. In His human nature, He could have had a wife and a family, as indicated in some ancient sources and non-canonical gospels.

Her objection came, 'Christ was without sin.'

To which I responded, 'According to Christianity, married life is not considered a sin.'

Furthermore, such Divine incarnations are beyond any custom or tradition and everything they do is for the benefit of others.

While in the midst of this conversation, we reached my destination. My host was waiting for me in a beautiful villa at the Palma, where she had her residence. We had many things to share about Guruji and about our wonderful monastery tour in Egypt which she had joined the year before.

The *yagna* was scheduled in a few days on the Diwali feast day. In the meantime, I suggested organising some more activities, but she emphasised that I should take time for myself. Since I was in Dubai for the first time, my host wanted me to experience the city from different angles. She showed me the downtown with all the skyscrapers and glamour, shopping malls and restaurants. We also went to the Indian quarter to visit the marketplace where she bought a beautiful Lakshmi *murti* for the *yagna* and *abhishekam*.

In general, Dubai appeared to be a place where many rich people were residing, but I felt that something essential was missing. This was 'the spirituality'.

In the afternoons, my host went to do some work while I was left to rest in her villa. As the house was situated directly on the seaside, I walked along the beach lined with opulent villas owned by politicians and eminent people from all over the world. Those places didn't seem to have good energy and so I returned to the house and waited for my host to come back.

In seeing all the material riches around me, I was glad to be a nun, living a simple life, and yet having everything I needed without owning it. As Guruji reminds us, 'Empty-handed we come into this world, and in the same way, we will leave one day empty-handed.' The only thing we take with us are our (good) deeds. Guruji often repeats not to attach to material things: 'Live in the world, but don't be from the world. Always remember that you are coming from God.'

The next morning, my host and I went to one of the best hotels in Dubai for breakfast. We found a nice place in front of the swimming pool area and started conversing about Gurudev. By simply talking about Him, it felt as though a spiritual field was created and spread around us.

As Guruji had stated that many lives are needed as a preparation to become ready to follow a *satguru*, I shared with my host how lucky we were to have Him and how empty and meaningless this life would be without Him. The involvement in His mission made this world appear colourful. The *satguru* is such a rare gift!

When I asked my host about the wood for the *yagna*, she looked at me puzzled, saying that wood was not available in the Emirates which is a desert country. This was something I didn't expect at all. I suggested collecting some tree branches in the desert outside Dubai, but she only laughed at that proposal. We had our first problem, but after many phone calls, we came upon a solution and ordered some grill wood which, in the end, worked perfectly.

On the day of Diwali, just before starting with the preparations for the *yagna*, another obstacle occurred. I, unexpectedly, got my period and so was neither allowed to prepare nor conduct the *yagna*. I didn't know what to do and messaged Guruji, suggesting several different options. He replied that my host should do the *yagna*.

Some days before, she had expressed her reluctance about wearing a *sari* or putting a *tilak* on her forehead. Now, she had only a few minutes to prepare herself as a *pujari*; to dress herself in my *sari* and to paint the *tilak*. We were both laughing at how Guruji works!

When some of her Indian friends called to confirm they were coming to participate in the *yagna*, they told her that they were bringing a *swami* with them who was a guide for the Indian community in Dubai. Upon hearing this, we became even more stressed.

As everyone arrived, we immediately engaged them in some service such as picking the flowers and preparing the garlands, painting the Lakshmi *murti*, setting up the *yagna* place, making up the *prasad* offering, or preparing the ingredients for the *abhishekam*. Everyone was busy and I was running around giving instructions. In spite of everything that was going on, we all enjoyed the service and finalised preparations just before the *swami* arrived.

As the ceremony started, I read the *mantras* and told my host what to do, while she followed the instructions calmly all the way to the very end.

After the *yagna*, we did Lakshmi *abhishekam* and sang *bhajans*, absorbed in the beautiful, divine energy. The whole event was a blessing and we felt the sweet presence of the Divine Mother.

The *swami* was pleased and invited us to continue with the Diwali celebration in a hotel with his followers. Guruji agreed to it, and three of us went to join the celebration which was a big party with around two hundred people.

When we arrived there, the *swami* asked me to give a talk on *bhakti*. Thinking that this was custom, and we all three had to speak on some topic, I just took the mic and started. Having talked and trembled in front of Guruji on several occasions, I could now talk in front of anyone.

Since his followers seemed to be worldly oriented, I spoke about the difference between *Pyaar*, the worldly, conditional love, and *Prema*, the divine, unconditional love, that Guruji often talks about, and the importance of having a spiritual teacher. Ultimately, this was an opportunity to introduce Guruji and to invite all to visit our *ashram* in Germany one day.

*****

One of my best times with Guruji was the trip to Macedonia.

The Mother I knew from there once visited our convent and *ashram* in Germany. During her stay, she invited us to return the visit and so, together with Guruji and one of His *swamis*, we went for a short monastery tour, to visit the Mother and some of Guruji's devotees from Macedonia.

During our journey, as we flew over the Balkans, Guruji looked at me and said, 'You have done a good job in these areas.'

As a *satguru*, He didn't need to say such things as our service should be selfless, and God and *guru* are the true doers. But still, His words were like a balm for the heart.

A wonderful sunny October day awaited us as we arrived in Macedonia. Two of Guruji's followers welcomed us at the airport, and while we were renting the car, Guruji materialised a ring for one of them. When everything was ready, we left and moved on towards the most beautiful Macedonian monasteries.

While the *swami* was driving fast, rushing to reach and visit the monasteries during the daylight, I enjoyed the rare opportunity to travel with Guruji in the car.

We reached the monasteries in time and were warmly welcomed by the monks and the clergy.

In one convent, the nuns recognised me from my past visit, and received Guruji with great respect. One of the nuns, as she looked at Guruji, remarked, 'Your eyes remind me of Christ's eyes.' The sisters joyfully told us about their newly established convent dedicated to the Most Holy

Theotokos in another part of Macedonia, which was celebrating a feast on the following day.

Overall, Guruji was pleased and very generous towards them, as usual. After a nice conversation, we left in order to reach our next destination and accommodation in time, which was a monastery on a lake.

On the way there we started talking about food, as we were already hungry. My hope was that some of the monasteries would invite us for dinner since they have excellent food, but they offered us only drinks and sweets. When I started praising the Macedonian food for the second time, Guruji emphasised, 'I am already waiting to taste this food.'

My last hope was that the monastery where we were staying overnight would offer some dinner. Otherwise, we would have to go to a restaurant where a great deal of meat was usually served.

When we arrived there, we found a beautiful monastery situated directly by the lake, with a small church and several caves of the ascetics from the past.

Only one servant was there, who welcomed us and was about to prepare some dinner.

Hungry and tired from the driving, the *swami* went to bed without a meal, and I stayed alone with Guruji in a large, majestic room for dinner. To my disappointment, as we sat down at the table, I noticed that the food was, unfortunately, out of the freezer and also contained egg. I made a face, but Guruji told me, with His eyes, not to behave that way and emphasised how good the pickles were, which was the only dish we could eat.

The next morning, we attended the liturgy and continued visiting monasteries around the large lake.

The lake was covered by a slight, whitish fog, while the light blue sky merged into the blue water, creating a mystic atmosphere. The place appeared like heaven on earth.

In one of the monasteries, we encountered a child-folklore group. I spontaneously asked them if they would perform for Guruji, and they agreed. With music playing from Guruji's phone, they danced the Macedonian folk dance just for Him. Guruji was very pleased with the children and invited the whole group for a drink in a nearby restaurant.

After visiting several monasteries, we proceeded towards the capital where a group of devotees and followers were waiting for us. As we were not in a hurry, Guruji spontaneously made a sign to leave the main road and to go towards a signposted monastery.

Following His instruction, we came to a narrow road leading through the forest up the mountain and, after a short drive, reached the monastery. As we entered the courtyard, I saw familiar faces, whereupon several nuns gathered joyfully around us, as if they knew us. And indeed, they were some of the sisters from the monastery the evening before. At that moment, I realised that we had 'coincidentally' arrived at their second convent dedicated to the Mother of God, which they had mentioned to us the day before. They immediately called us to join their feast in a big hall filled with guests.

Just a few minutes after we had sat down, strong church bells started ringing. People looked at each other wondering, and even the nuns did not seem to know what was going on. The bells would only ring when their bishop was approaching.

We all rushed outside to greet the bishop, but no one had arrived.

After a few minutes, the abbess asked us to return, since it was a false alarm, or some 'confused nun'.

We stayed with them for tea and cake and, after Guruji had spent some time with them, we bade farewell to one another. The moment we reached the courtyard, the bells started to ring again. People were coming out of the buildings not knowing what was happening. The whole place appeared mesmerised, and everyone followed Guruji as we entered the car and left.

It was a majestic experience. Perhaps Mother Mary had her own way of greeting Guruji? In the car, He just commented, 'Do you see that God arranges everything!'

We reached the capital late, but Guruji was very pleased with the lovely welcome from the devotees and followers.

We stayed overnight at Mother's beautiful convent, which Guruji deeply admired, chatting with her until late into the night.

Guruji mentioned later that this country had the most loving monastics, who welcomed Him in the most respectful way. We enjoyed their simplicity and their calm.

This trip was one of the greatest material gifts I have ever received from Guruji.

# The Process

In 2013 our spiritual centre and *ashram was* officially opened.

The building was very well renovated and arranged with loving attention to detail, while the green area around the *ashram was* transformed into a flourishing park. Many devotees and followers contributed to this accomplishment.

Guruji, who was elevated to the status of a *Mahamandaleshwar* (the highest level of Hindu spiritual guardianship), started initiating many *swamis* and *swaminis*, who in turn initiated new devotees. The initiation procedure was slightly reformed and adjusted to the needs of people and time. Worldwide, numerous Bhakti Marga centres were opening. Most of them were dedicated to Narasimha, since His energy was best suitable to handle and transform the negativity which both humanity and our planet are going through. A large crowd from near and far started following Guruji and visiting our centre. The number of residents, and with the organisation itself, was growing rapidly. Bhakti Marga was blossoming.

The *yoga* and meditation department where I had my *seva* was very busy. Our small initial team had developed a good framework to build upon in the following years. Various trainings, workshops and meetings were developed and organised, as well as teaching materials.

OM Chanting established a solid foundation with a family spirit. It spread like fire across the globe by Guruji's grace. The participants would experience profound insights, healings, revelations or visions during OM Chanting. They loved it and many were eager to start their own circles.

Over the years, several changes and challenges happened in our department and in the *ashram* in general. Those situations were teaching us flexibility, better teamwork and, at the same time, were offering opportunities for inner transformation. Sometimes it appeared that certain circumstances were purposely arranged in a most difficult way so that we could learn the most from it, to crush our egos and to become humbler.

Throughout the years, Guruji emphasised humility as a crucial quality for spiritual advancement. He stressed that spiritual pride was the worst enemy and that one could lose everything through it. On a few occasions, He called attention to my own pride and told me to keep a watchful eye on it.

In my past, I often mistook humility as weakness. At a young age, I learned to fight for my rights and not to allow myself to be suppressed. Only after starting on the spiritual path, did I realise how important and powerful humility actually was. Along with patience, it carries enormous spiritual strength and blessing.

Once, I had a dream in which I was praying to the Divine Mother. I was lifted upwards through different levels. The first was the level of angels where pride still existed. The second was the level of knowledge where people were highly knowledgeable but still full of themselves. Last was the level where people were humble, selflessly serving others. I clearly recognised this third level as the highest.

In 2015, during the tenth anniversary of Bhakti Marga and the first Just Love Festival, Guruji reminded me of the need for humility. A special book was prepared for this event detailing the development of Bhakti Marga and Guruji's mission over the past ten years. The residents were asked to contribute a short story about Guruji, which would be included into the book along with many pictures and descriptions of different events that took place with Him.

I wrote my story, mentioning my vocation as a nun, and was very enthusiastic about it. When the book was published, with its voluminous, colourful pages, we all admired it. It was beautifully arranged, with numerous pictures of Guruji, festivities and events. In between, there were the stories of the residents with their pictures.

I flipped through the book and could neither find my story, nor a single picture of me. Everyone was included, even those who joined Bhakti Marga just a short time ago. But I, who had spent all those years with Guruji, was nowhere in the book. Having such thoughts, I felt something churn inside of me, but I eventually calmed myself down and went to the festival's opening.

The Just Love Festival, held on the ashram grounds, invited people from all over the world to enjoy spiritual music and celebrate the Divine Name. It started with a presentation of the last ten years of Bhakti Marga on a huge music stage. The presenter reviewed the course of time, mostly mentioning the achievements of the *prabhus*. *Matajis* were hardly mentioned, and there was not a single trace of my *seva* contribution alluded to. It appeared as if I didn't exist in those ten years.

After the presentation, I approached the presenter and told him about it. He explained that the presentation was prepared by someone else and advised me to talk to him. When I saw that person, I told him about my concerns, addressing my lack of inclusion in the book as well. He calmly replied that my story was excluded because I mentioned being a nun. As far as the pictures were concerned, he explained that he was not checking on who was or wasn't in them.

This issue stayed on my mind throughout the rest of that day and into the next.

On the following day, I was sitting near the stage while the festival boomed with crowds all around. Guruji passed by and, seeing me, asked how I was. As spontaneously as a child, I told Him that I was sad about the fact that I was not in any of the presentation pictures. He seemed to be in a hurry, but before He walked away, He gave me a stern look which left the impression that this was not the end of the story.

The next day, when Guruji publicly performed *puja* on stage to His Giridhari, I was standing among the audience in the front rows. When the *puja* finished and Guruji was walking down the stage, I tried to step back a little bit, not wanting to be too close to Him. Since hundreds of people were behind me and were crowding forward, it was impossible for me to move.

Passing by, Guruji stopped directly in front of me and with a firm look asked, 'Tell me, why do you want your picture to be shown?' He paused and went on, 'Have you forgotten what humility is?' After saying this, He left disappointedly.

I felt ashamed and with a bowed head went to sit alone and process the experience. It was hard to be scolded by Guruji, but at the same time, it was a blessing. The mind was still again, and the delusion was removed. I could clearly see that I wanted recognition, and because of that desire, my service was not selfless. The mindset was egoistic and Guruji had to interfere.

The following day, I met a *swami* whose story was also not included in the book. When I asked him about his opinion, he said, 'Behind all these situations is ultimately Him (Guruji) giving us a learning opportunity.'

I understood that the whole situation was an opportunity to transform pride. It was not about fairness, but about humility on my part.

*****

2017 marked ten-years since Guruji and Babaji gave Atma Kriya Yoga to the world. To celebrate this occasion, I started planning 'The International Days of OM Chanting' with the team from the *yoga* and meditation department. My assistant and I were enthusiastically organising and managing 500+ registrations from more than 40 different countries for this event.

Shortly before beginning to plan this event, our team was assigned a new area manager. Even though we had been working together for many years, he was not happy with our team, stressing that other departments were complaining about us. Specifically, I was reproached for pushing others and busying them unnecessarily in my aspiration to achieve an ideal result.

This claim was partly true since not everyone in the *ashram* had the same attitude towards their *seva* duties. Often, it was necessary for me to remind somebody of their task so that the whole process could continue moving forward.

In light of this dynamic, some more difficult situations developed during the preparations for the 'International Days' celebration. We were asked to organise several tasks through another manager, who, to our surprise, didn't follow up on those tasks until shortly before the event. As a result, many changes and adjustments were made at the last moment. With only a few days before the event, the area manager passed the project lead from me to my assistant. The whole situation got so complicated that, by the end, I succumbed to my weakness and lost my calm. I just wanted to get the event over with.

Fortunately, on the morning of the event someone showed me a picture of Guruji wearing a t-shirt with the 'International Days of OM Chanting' design we had prepared for all the participants. After seeing this, I gathered myself and went, with a smile, to meet all the people with whom I had worked together for so many years.

It was heart-warming to see all the OM Chanting Organisers – all those who had received the blessing to lead OM Chanting circles – arriving from all over the world, making all efforts to participate, share and celebrate together. The event had a varied programme: Guruji gave a beautiful Satsang, in which He expressed His gratitude to the organisers and revealed new benefits of this healing method. We had workshops and presentations, a huge OM Chanting circle with all of the event participants and, in the end, a beautiful celebration. The entire event was a successful coming together of a big and strong family.

Several days after the event ended, I was called by our area manager for a serious conversation, where I felt that my *seva* with OM Chanting was coming to an end. Our department was in the process of being completely restructured and I couldn't contribute much anymore. I asked Guruji for His advice, and after some days, He gave His blessing to leave the department. The travels to spread OM Chanting would continue and I would also have more time to dedicate to the convent.

Unexpectedly, it was at this time that a series of signs began to occur that indicated a twist of fate.

During a Bhakti Marga event, an astrologer devotee visited our centre and offered to make a chart for me. I knew that Guruji didn't want us to rely on horoscopes, especially because the destiny and the life of a devotee is in the hands of the Guru.

However, I took it more as entertainment and agreed to it.

When she read my chart, she intuitively and precisely gave indications. I was surprised and interested when she asked me if I had chosen to become a nun, as this was not in accordance with my chart. She also told me about 'my longing to have a family'. I explained to her that Bhakti Marga was my family and that the *satguru* can change things in our lives.

Nevertheless, she predicted that in the upcoming year something significant would happen and that I would be sent on a mission to a far-off country. A new period would begin where I could put everything into practice that I had learned in my life. She mentioned Mother Teresa and reaching out to many people. Interestingly, she also said that, according to the chart, I would have a child in this life. With that, our conversation ended, and I tried not to think too much about it.

Around the same time, Guruji came to me in a dream announcing that some event was going to happen and that I would go through a difficult time.

Another time, I dreamt about the convent and 'where I would stop, another *mataji* would continue one day'.

In a separate dream, I saw myself as a nun, running with a torch in my hand, trying to reach some destination. I was suddenly shot from behind, and as I fell dead to the ground, I managed to pass the torch to another person.

Eventually, I even received the following vision: the world map appeared again, but this time it was the land of bananas and elephants, which I recognised to be India. I saw myself talking to people and a scene with children who were calling me saying, 'We want you to be our mummy.'

These events were confusing, and I didn't know what to expect in light of them. It was clear to me, however, that something would happen soon.

# The End of the Convent

The convent life was challenging. It seemed that there was not enough passion and commitment to build a sisterhood, to hold the convent together and to sustain it over time. Most of us were going through our own intense processes. The convent was a small community within a larger, Bhakti Marga community and so we had to be flexible and able to adjust to different situations. Furthermore, it was not a direct part of Guruji's mission.

After the opening of our new *ashram* temple in 2018, the church of Bhakti Marga became even more dormant. On one occasion, Guruji told me that His love for Christ, Mother Mary and the saints will always remain, but the church would not understand our path. He advised me to continue with the convent as long as it was possible, but that His focus would no longer be on it. He also suggested that I, along with another sister, undertake another pilgrimage to Egypt where we could visit several monasteries.

With the support of the Mother from Cairo, we planned a monastery tour in Upper Egypt. The church helped us gain official permission for our pilgrimage, since the Christian holy places were potential terrorist targets.

The sister and I went to Cairo first. We visited several holy places and stayed at the Cairo convent with the Mother and her sisterhood. The convent was a spiritually vibrant place and we felt very welcomed there. Despite being in her sixties, the Mother looked very young, with a joyful, childish spirit and a deep wisdom. We had beautiful and funny moments together, talking with admiration about the saints and the places we were about to visit.

During our first day there, we visited nearby churches which are witnesses of a great history and sainthood. One of them was the Monastery of Saint Barsoum. We had a lovely gathering with the sisters there and enjoyed their company until late. Already at the end of our first day in Egypt, we felt so fulfilled and blessed that we wondered how we would continue on in the remaining days.

From Cairo, we took a plane to Sohag where we met a devotee of Guruji living in Egypt, as well as our driver and guide. With all five of us together in a car, we travelled along the Nile through Aswan and Luxor towards Asyut, visiting ancient monasteries and holy places, meeting several bishops, and taking blessings from the saints or saintly people.

Everywhere we went, we were welcomed with a sisterly love, given a guided tour around the particular place we were visiting, a meal, a refreshment, and/or some gifts. After some days, our driver became desperate: we had collected so many gifts that he was not able to place them in the car anymore and eventually we had to hold them on our knees. It was a happy time together full of laughter, singing, and talking about our spiritual father.

In one monastery, we met an old nun who completely covered herself, including her hands and face. Light literally beamed from her hands which was the reason she wore gloves. While she was physically blind, it was clear that she could see more clearly than others who had their eyesight.

At another place, we met an elder who was immersed in devotion for Christ. With tears in his eyes and a child-like innocence, he distributed pictures of saints to us. At the end of our time together, instead of him blessing us, he asked us for a blessing. It was lovely to be in the company of the devotees of Christ.

We went to the Monastery of Virgin Mary in Koskam to visit the Church of the Virgin which was built over an ancient cave. This is where Mary and Jesus had spent six months during their flight to Egypt from King Herod. We also visited St. Mary Monastery on Mount Dronka, which was the last stop before the Holy Family headed to Cairo and then back to Israel. The presence of the Divine

Mother was so strong in these places that we bathed in Her sweetness.

Egypt is a special place which has kept its monasticism vivid, humble, and passionate for God and His saints.

After we visited The White and The Red Monasteries, which were both previously ancient pharaonic temples that were later transformed into churches, I was left touched by their unique combination of culture and religion. One could feel the layers of centuries charged with different energies, overlapping one another. Out of curiosity, I wrote Guruji and asked about His opinion on pharaonic spirituality and tradition.

He answered, 'It was for that time, and it finished when Jesus came there.'

His words brought a new insight to me: that a religion serves a purpose to humanity for a certain time, and that with the coming of Christ to Egypt, pharaonic spirituality was replaced with something more suitable for human evolution. There seemed to be a 'religious update' (evolution) in accordance with the time and needs of the people.

I wrote back to Guruji, 'Will some present religions also end one day?'

He replied, 'Yes.'

When we reached the Dronka Monastery, my fellow sister left for Germany. The Egyptian devotee and I stayed there three more days, enjoying the silence and the love of Mother Mary with each breath.

At this point, I asked Guruji about my *ishtadeva*. Having never openly revealed my *ishtadeva* to me, He had advised me to take the aspect of God I felt most close to. On this day, however, He answered, 'It's Krishna.'

This was a surprise to me since I assumed all those years that it was Christ.

To this, Guruji answered, 'That's why I never told you. But it is up to you to follow what you want.'

His words made me think and I further inquired, 'Guruji was it my *dharma* to become a Christian nun?'

To my astonishment He answered, 'Wish only.'

He disclosed something unexpected which continued to work on me in the time following this conversation.

I returned to Cairo and spent one more day in the convent with the Mother.

Before my departure, an orthodox woman from Switzerland visited us. She was eager to meet me and find out more about my monastic background. The difference between people who were following Christ' teachings in their hearts and those who were following religious doctrines in their minds was clear to me. This woman belonged to the second group.

After our conversation, she remained suspicious and started searching for more information about our convent in Germany. It was a few weeks later, after I came back from a trip to Slovenia, that I received a voice message on my phone. It was the Swiss woman requesting me not to contact the convent in Cairo any longer as she had found out about my connection to Bhakti Marga.

There were many obstacles on our monastic path since it was unusual and incomprehensible for most people, but that day I knew it was the time for a change. I sent Guruji a message and He called me back, asking for more details. During our talk, I mentioned my readiness to live again as a *brahmacharini*, as it seemed to be the best solution.

Later that evening, Guruji messaged me that it was time to 'end this part' and focus on our Hindu path because people would not be able to understand. He explained that the convent church would remain, and we could continue with the prayers, but we needed to all go back to being *brahmacharinis* again.

Guruji knew what was best and with that, the official time of the convent ended after 6 years.

# The Charity

The Bhakti Marga movement, with all its spiritual activities, is a huge charity for humanity. It transforms the lives of people and makes this world a better place. In the years 2007 and 2008, Bhakti Marga started some additional humanitarian projects. Guruji asked the countries with a strong community of devotees to initiate charitable activities according to the needs of their areas. However, this was not one of the more important aspects of Bhakti Marga at the time, and so these initiatives eventually dwindled until they were discontinued altogether.

I felt very attracted to the charity work and, on a few occasions throughout the years, asked Guruji if it was the right time to continue with it. His answer was always 'no' or 'not yet'.

A little while after leaving the *yoga* and meditation department, I messaged Guruji and mentioned that, if He wanted to restart the charity work, I would be glad to support it. A week later, Guruji called me over and said, 'Go on with your charity.'

It was an honour to receive this direction from Him and I was eager to begin. On that same day, I informed a *swami* about it and we talked about how best to proceed. Later, we met with our general manager and initiated regular meetings to work together on a vision and mission statement.

The main idea was to begin with local humanitarian activities in different countries, whereby the devotees could cultivate both the *sangha* and selfless service. In addition, I planned to go to South India for the opening of the charity project started by the lady from Oman and which had already been blessed by Guruji.

Over time, the launching of the charity work within Bhakti Marga led to an ever-increasing discussion amongst the leadership. The situation became more complex and the topic most sensitive. On the advice of a *swami*, I stepped back from the project for a while. Even if Guruji encouraged me to continue with the charity, there was no official permission for it.

After the convent ended, I lost some ground under my feet and felt disoriented. Little by little, resentment started growing inside of me and I withdrew myself more from the community. The permanent crowds in the *ashram* started annoying me and a doubt and judgement subtly found a place in my mind. During moments of anger, I realised the danger of spiritual power with an uncontrolled mind. The more we advance, the more we can harm ourselves or others through negative thoughts and actions, and the greater our downfall can be.

As Guruji stated many times, we need to first purify and make ourselves ready to receive what He has come to give us. This was a time when I couldn't see and appreciate what I had but which, on the other hand, presented me with an opportunity for deeper transformation.

After the situation had created a distance towards Guruji and the community, I started reminding myself that whatever we are going through in life, it is guided by God and *guru* and that it happens for a reason. Even if we don't perceive the situation, a devotee has to trust. The organisation is also an extension of the *guru*, who appointed certain people for specific functions, and we need to respect His lead. Maybe it was just not the right time to start the charity and I could, perhaps, do something else?

On the advice of a *swami*, I sent Guruji a message, asking if there was something else He wanted me to do for Bhakti Marga that was in accordance with His will, my *dharma* and my qualities. He replied, 'Yes. I want you to go and serve for three months in Delhi at AIIMS (All India Institutes for Medical Sciences).'

I knew that there was a charity project run by Bhakti Marga India at AIIMS hospital in New Delhi and immediately agreed to it. But what would I do there for three months?

I asked Guruji about it and He responded, 'They need someone to look after them and to console them. Many children there have cancer.'

I was glad that there was a clear instruction coming from Him. The general plan was to go for two weeks to Tamil Nadu for the opening of the new charity project and to proceed to Delhi for the charity work at AIIMS. Guruji mentioned that He would arrange for my stay.

On one evening, during a Satsang in the garden, Guruji was talking about Bishma and how he took a tremendous vow on himself. He explained that certain decisions in life are like an arrow. Once it is shot, there is no return and it must proceed towards its target.

Hearing this, the suspicion arose within myself that the charity initiative might be an arrow which I have shot, and which was actually just my own wish. After the Satsang, I approached Guruji with a question, mentioning Bishma and my concern about the charity.

He looked at me angrily, and like a consuming fire, told me, 'Who do you think you are! You think only of yourself!'

Before I could say anything, He pointed with His index finger to leave the place. To my greater embarrassment, people were standing around witnessing this exchange. It didn't matter anymore though, as it was high time to let go of what others thought of me. I walked away trying to stay aware and calm. I knew that if the mind took over in such a moment, it could be my downfall and reminded myself that His scolding was some kind of blessing in disguise.

I went to the Panduranga *mandir* (temple), as it was my turn for *arati*, and the tears just started rolling. The sister *pujari* asked me what had happened. I could only reply that Guruji had been strict with me.

Just when the *arati* finished, Guruji came inside. Upon seeing Him, I wished to fall at His feet and cry. Instead, I stayed in the corner, silent.

When He saw me, He objected, 'Why are you asking me such a question about past lives? You know that I don't like it.'

I looked at Him, wondering what He meant, and repeated my question, 'Not about past lives. About charity. If it was my wish, and therefore, You are sending me to India.'

He replied, 'No, I am sending you because I want you to go there, and I will take care of the rest.'

After He had said this, He left the *mandir* and I felt some relief.

The sister *pujari* commented, 'He was so gentle to you.'

I wearily replied, 'But you don't know what He told me before.'

After this incident, I reflected on my relationship with Guruji. I always longed to be physically closer to Him and all my efforts went towards achieving this aim. Consequently, my inner focus became less, and this exchange was a reminder to focus on cultivating my inner relationship with Him more. Physical closeness to Guruji without a strong inner connection to Him could be a fragile position to be in, and I decided to give more attention to that part of our relationship.

# In India

At first my journey took me to a small village in Tamil Nadu, South India, where the opening of the charity project by the lady from Oman took place. I did not know what would await me there, but the plan was to organise some OM Chanting circles with the villagers.

The opening included the inauguration of the *seva* centre along with a Shirdi Sai Baba *murti* and a celebration in which some prominent personalities took part. The centre was meant to offer different activities for the villagers that would support their personal and spiritual development, as well as their health. It was a new and nicely arranged venue, managed with love and care by the family from Oman.

My arrival in India was marked with anxiety. After fourteen years of *ashram* life, I was afraid of falling back into the ways of the world and becoming involved in mundaneness. When living in the spiritual setting of Bhakti Marga, it was easy to be strong. I didn't know how the world would influence me over an extended period of time and I was concerned that the old *samskaras* could take over. Since there was no longer an outer spiritual anchor, I had to find it more from within.

To focus myself better on Guruji, besides doing Atma Kriya Yoga and *japa*, I started performing a short *puja* to His *padukas* (house shoes) and reciting His 108 names. The *padukas* were my main object of worship and I carried them with me during my travels whenever possible. When anxiety would come up, I would use the names of Guruji as a sword to destroy the enemy and would feel peaceful again.

After the inauguration of the *seva* centre, we started practising OM Chanting twice a day with both the adults and the children. In the morning, my host had *yoga* lessons with the adults while I did OM Chanting with the children. In the evening it was the opposite. The children were especially sweet and affectionate. With their big dark eyes, they would innocently look at me and ask questions, curious about what we would do together.

The weather was pleasantly warm with an occasional breeze and after the OM Chanting, we would go for a walk or sing and dance together. Spending time with the children was heart opening. I was not only there for them, but they were also there for me. Their presence was sweet and soothing and, for the first time, I felt that these were 'my children'.

One evening during the *puja* to Shirdi Sai Baba, we all spontaneously gathered to sing *bhajans*. The group was enthusiastic and passionate. We enjoyed the singing until late and they wondered at how a European lady knew their tradition.

While there were many aspects of the culture which I found beautiful, I couldn't help being struck by the vast amount of waste in the village (and all over India) that was scattered on all sides of the streets, in the courtyards and all along the riverbanks. One day I asked the children why they were throwing their rubbish everywhere. They answered that it was because there were no waste bins on the streets.

With the help of the lady from Oman, we organised a gathering with the village elder, the village president, and some of the villagers. I prepared a talk about cleanliness and how it related to material and spiritual abundance. At the end, I asked all of those in attendance if they wanted to begin taking steps towards having a more clean and pleasant environment. They all affirmed that they did, and we decided to start some local clean-up activities.

On the very next day, around twelve women met at a desolate, though beautiful, ancient Shiva temple in their village. We started with weeding and picking up the waste all around the temple complex. Despite the heat, the women were diligent and committed to their task. Their simplicity, cheerful mood and motherly care reminded me of the *gopis*. They brought snacks and drinks to share with one another and would come and place some of their delicacies in my mouth. The collective spirit was strong, and we continued cleaning together in the following days.

As a next step, my host made an agreement with the villagers to purchase and install the needed waste bins on the streets. In the meantime, I visited the village schools and organised OM Chanting there. A few people were trained and received the blessing to be able to lead OM Chanting groups so that the practice could continue after my departure. I was warmly welcomed everywhere I went.

On my last day at this village, all the ladies each brought a dish for a festive lunch in the *seva* centre. As a farewell, we ate together and enjoyed the excellent South Indian specialties. And with that, the first part of my *seva* was completed.

From there, a lovely family from Coimbatore invited me to stay at their place for a few days to introduce OM Chanting and organise some spiritual gatherings in their community. After that, my next destination was Kerala, where I would visit some Christian monasteries. It was at this point that I contacted Guruji to ask Him for His blessing.

He inquired how my journey in the South was going, mentioning that if things would become difficult for me at AIIMS, I could go back to the South and continue with the *seva* there. He had already received some pictures from the charity project and was pleased with the development.

I was glad to help patients at AIIMS but expressed to Him my concern about getting lost in the world. It was mostly that I felt scared because of some strange dreams. Guruji just replied, 'Focus on your service.'

By communicating with Him, I felt His presence and blessing enveloping me.

In those moments He was invisibly with me, walking next to me and even carrying me if it was necessary, but I needed to also stand on my own feet. Once again, I felt encouraged, guided and guarded by Him to continue with my time in India.

# In Delhi

I arrived at the Delhi airport in the evening and was welcomed by two of the Bhakti Marga sisters from Vrindavan. They came to show me to my apartment and to tell me everything I needed to know as I began my time in the city.

Delhi was not a place where I would have ever chosen to live due, in large part, to the masses of people, the permanent traffic, the constant honking and the waste all around. On top of this, it happened to be the monsoon season which made conditions extremely hot, humid and difficult to breathe in. Nevertheless, I remembered the wise saying, 'Bloom where you are planted.'

My apartment was in a nice area of Delhi, just five kilometres from AIIMS. One of the sisters from Vrindavan told me that she had been guided by Guruji to find it. The apartment itself was modest and had all the furnishings I needed. By arranging the altar and placing some holy pictures around, a pleasant living atmosphere was easily created.

On that evening I poured my heart out to the sisters about my uncertainty regarding what Guruji wanted from me. It felt as though He was sending me away for some new and unknown step in my life. I clearly still had some turmoil inside of me and it was apparent that only time held the answers I was looking for.

On the following day, one of the Vrindavan sisters and I took the metro to AIIMS. As we walked up to street level from the underground metro, we faced a broad, overcrowded street with small shops and pharmacies, one after the other, lining the road and leaving an unpleasant smell in the air.

AIIMS is a large complex of various buildings and units. As it offered the best medical treatments in India, individuals and families from different parts of the country and with all kinds of conditions found their way there. In addition to the hospital, there was also a shelter home for the poorest patients and their families on the AIIMS premises.

After passing several guards, we reached a long barracks building. Some children readily came towards us, and the sister from Vrindavan greeted them nicely in Hindi. When we went inside, we found a long hall with mattresses arranged on both sides, leaving a small path in the middle for walking through. Within the two square metres of their individual living space, people were sitting, lying down or eating.

We greeted everyone and sat down next to a young lady who was paralysed. Some more children gathered around us and held our hands or sat in our laps. The sister introduced me and after a short chat, we started singing *bhajans* together. The children were clapping or dancing, and the ladies sitting around turned in our direction to join us from where they were.

Although the shelter was very dirty and was filled with sick people, being there instantly touched my heart. The atmosphere was imbued with acceptance; people were living in the present moment and the children, though sick, were cheerful.

The place sheltered individuals and families for both short and long periods. Most of them were patients who were receiving some type of regular therapy at AIIMS or were waiting for surgery or a diagnosis.

Many of the children had leukaemia or some other kind of cancer and were staying there for a longer period of time with their family. In other cases, the parents were sick, and the children followed them. Some of the people were homeless because they had sold everything they owned in order to finance their treatments.

Several volunteers were regularly visiting the shelter home to help support the people with medicine and basic needs. Bhakti Marga India was among the volunteers who provided for the needs of the children.

Right at the beginning, I noticed that the children did not attend school and that most of the people had head lice. In the following days, a volunteer informed me about the afternoon school on the premises of AIIMS where the children could join. Its founder was a nice lady who gladly agreed to welcome all the children who were five years old and older.

The school was outside in an open area underneath a huge tree. The children sat in small groups according to their age and prior knowledge and were guided by a teacher.

The first step was to motivate the children to attend the school and to make their parents aware of the importance of their education. To achieve this, I started coming to the shelter home every day before the school would begin, to call the children together and bring them to the school. Later, I would leave to do something else and would come back in the evening to organise a short OM Chanting and take them to their shelter home.

In spite of my inability to speak Hindi and their inability to speak English, we could still communicate with very few words by using gestures and facial expressions. Most of them didn't receive much attention from their parents, who were coping with the hardships of life. As a result, they were affectionate and thrilled that someone cared for them. I too enjoyed their company. Even with something as simple as a walk, I would hold the hand of two children in each one of my hands while the other children would walk holding onto my *sari*.

In the beginning I was bringing some simple gifts for the children as they were lacking so many things. Consequently, they would show such greedy behaviour which resulted in them fighting with each other. These behaviours obviously didn't serve the educational and spiritual purposes we were trying to foster. I felt that, next to the medical provision for the children, our focus should be to support them with education and establish the right human values within them.

Since there was no free space for any additional activities within the shelter home, I requested a room from AIIMS. They approved and allowed us to use a small room twice a week where we organised painting activities for the children, breathing exercises and meditation for the cancer patients, and English lessons for everyone.

While it was easy to communicate with the children, it took much more effort to communicate with the adults. I spoke English with a few Sanskrit and Hindi words, in between a lot of gestures. Accordingly, their facial expressions often communicated their own puzzlement at my efforts. Yet, with a lot of intuition and improvisation it was possible and beautiful to practise together.

By far, the most precious activity we did together was the spiritual singing. This was a unique gift that soothed the hearts and souls of people, especially in the moments where it was obvious that their life and death were in the hands of God and that everything depended on His grace. On some days we would sing with such a passion that we literally felt His grace descending upon us. The shelter home would transform into a temple! As Guruji had emphasised so many times: God and His Name are the same. The *Hanuman-chalisa*, in particular, was the biggest attraction for the children. Little by little, our main spiritual nourishment became the Holy Name.

Once, when I came to the shelter home, two youngsters were in terrible pain. I didn't know what to do or how to help them and was just softly singing God's Name while sitting next to them. The peaceful vibration started to spread, and the youngsters calmed down.

Another time, a woman was beating her head from pain. I sat next to her and repeated the *mantra* '*om namo narayanaya*' for half an hour. She repeated it after me by herself and calmed down immediately. Later she continued using this *mantra*.

To the people who were very sick or close to death, Guruji allowed me to whisper a *mantra* in their ear. He once wrote to me, 'Bring love to all of them, whether they live or not…'

There was a seven-year-old girl named Raani whom we met in the shelter home on my first day there who touched my heart. Ever since her brain inflammation, which had happened a year and a half earlier, she and her mother spent most of their time at the AIIMS hospital. When we first met Raani, we sang her the *bhajan* 'Radharani Ki Jai' and from then on, she would address me with, 'Radhe Radhe, Didi', calling me with excitement to sing together.

Half of Raani's body was paralysed and so she had to be in a wheelchair. Additionally, she had become overweight due to the strong medications she had to take. It was touching to see her young and cheerful mother, selflessly taking care of her under the most difficult circumstances. Her husband was in Bihar with their other two children but visited them regularly.

Like many other patients, Raani was waiting for an adequate treatment or surgery. Occasionally, she would start losing awareness, at which point her mother would shake her and she would regain consciousness again. Most of the time, however, she just slept.

As a result of living in unfavourable conditions for an extended period of time, Raani eventually developed a lung infection and a severe cough. At last, she was admitted to the intensive care unit within the hospital.

Visiting her regularly in the intensive care unit, I naturally encountered many other children in extremely critical conditions; children, whose lives the doctors were fervently fighting for. In some cases, it was even more striking to observe the parents who, while in shock, found themselves in an utterly helpless situation.

Something was pulling me to spend time with these parents. After taking the children from the shelter home to the school, I started going to the hospital. The medical staff was tolerant since the parents welcomed me as their guest. I felt that encouraging or embracing a desperate mother, uncertain of her child's survival, was a meaningful service to render. Sometimes we prayed together, or I would chant a Vedic hymn. When it became evident that the child would not survive, I would ask for permission to chant the *mantra* in the child's ear.

It was sad on some days to encounter an empty bed or to see a new child lying where another child had been. By some grace, I kept the awareness that the soul is immortal. While the body made of the five elements remains lifeless, the spirit moves on passing into another existence. For the parents, however, who had a strong relationship and attachment to their child, it was a very painful process.

One evening when I was about to leave the shelter home, Raani's mother came in crying. She said that her daughter was experiencing severe breathing problems and was now attached to an oxygen mask. We went to the hospital together where I saw the poor child gasping for breath, while her parents were taking turns holding the mask above her face. I didn't know how to help and was just standing next to her, softly singing her favourite song.

It seemed that Raani's body was severely affected and would not serve her much longer. I sent Guruji a message about it, and shortly after, He replied, 'I shall be with her.' My assumption was that she would pass away and that He would take care of her.

When the doctor asked me to leave, I looked around and noticed other parents struggling for the lives of their children. It was like being in a dream. Those moments reminded me of how fragile life really is.

When I went to see Raani the next day she was hooked up to artificial respiration. Due to pain, she was trying to pull the tubes out from her nostrils and mouth. Her mother had to hold her hands in order to prevent her from doing that and she asked me to take her place with Raani for a moment.

When I took Raani's hands, she immediately fixed her eyes straight on the pendant around my neck with Guruji's image. I noticed that she became calm and so I let go of her hands. She grasped the pendant, looking first at Guruji's picture, and then she turned it over to see the Vaishnava *tilak* on the other side.

When we saw her doing this, her mother and I looked at one other with a questioning gaze. A moment later, Raani started fidgeting again and, since I had to leave, her mother took over. This was the last time I saw Raani.

The following day it was not possible to visit her due to the heavy monsoon rain. The next day, as I was on the way to the hospital, the message reached me that Raani had passed away. Somehow, I sensed that this would happen and was glad that Guruji knew about her condition.

When I arrived at AIIMS, the parents were waiting in the ambulance in front of the entrance. The mother was beside herself, crying bitterly. They wanted me to see their daughter for the last time before the cremation: Raani, the sweet little girl who was sleeping peacefully on the stretcher inside the ambulance.

Another volunteer arrived and we took Raani's mother with us, supporting her to help pull herself together. After a while, she calmed down and slowly started packing the suitcases. Her long stay at the shelter home had ended with the passing of her child.

That night, when I returned home and closed my eyes to sleep, a short, bright vision appeared: Raani was joyfully smiling, wearing a hairband with white bunny ears. The image disappeared after a few seconds, and I opened my eyes in the dark room. Usually, I would be afraid of a vision like this but on this occasion the experience was actually pleasing. I understood that she was happy, and that Guruji had brought her to a nice place.

*****

My time in Delhi was passing quickly. Besides the service at AIIMS, I also had my own personal spiritual program. In the morning I practised Atma Kriya Yoga, performed *puja* and listened to the *Vishnusahasranama*. On Sundays, I joined the liturgy at the Syriac Orthodox Church, and occasionally visited the ISKCON temple to immerse myself more into the Divine Name.

In general, I felt good and protected, and did not miss anything other than Guruji and fresh air.

While being physically far away from Guruji, His presence was strong around me. The altar with His *padukas* was next to my bed. On some nights I would place my hands on them and fall asleep.

One night when I closed my eyes to sleep, I saw radiant dark blue feet. In amazement I looked up to see the rest of His body, but He was so huge that I could not see Him in totality. I woke up with my hands holding on to His *padukas*.

Another time, I had a similar experience after closing my eyes, but I perceived a little bluish child on a leaf. As this vision was occurring, I could not grasp the meaning behind it. Upon opening my eyes, it came to my mind that I had placed a small *murti* of baby Krishna, whom I had bought for performing *puja* with the children, in one of Guruji's *padukas*. It was such a sweet insight of who Guruji might be.

During my stay in Delhi there were phases where my mind questioned things. Was I sent to India for some mission or was it because I could not handle life in the *ashram*? Why was it so challenging for me in the *ashram* in recent years? Was it necessary to close the convent? Had I failed? Did I miss some important chance?

My attempts to see a bigger picture were in vain and I tried my best to remember that devotees do not worry. Instead, devotees accept everything as a gift from God and trust in His inner guidance.

One evening I remembered the convent and all the blessings and opportunities Guruji had given us. The memories were still painful. I felt a grudge towards some people and tried to find forgiveness within myself. Feeling pain well up in my chest, I cried that night remembering different situations. Through those tears, a relief came with an understanding that we are simply humans who still make mistakes. I was determined to focus on projects where I was needed or accepted and made a resolution to accept people as they are.

After a few miserable days, I woke up with the words, 'It is on you to move forward in life.' When I contemplated them, I felt that Guruji was giving me a new responsibility in India. The children in the shelter home were more than happy to have someone who cared for them. Ultimately, I was still a 'mother' but in a different way, and for many more people than in the convent.

One morning, when the mind was dominant again, I was thinking how easily we are forgotten by people. I had been living in the *ashram* for many years, but since leaving for India, it was rare that anyone from there contacted me. With such a mindset, I opened my phone and was amazed to see a message from Guruji. He wrote, 'How is everything there, how are the children?'

I was overwhelmed seeing it, and at the same time, felt embarrassed for my judging mind. This was another reminder that even if the whole world forgets us, which will inevitably happen after leaving this physical plane, the *satguru* will never forget us. We can only forget Him. Even still, He will continue guiding us in different ways, patiently awaiting our return. Family and friends will come and go as they are restricted to this life, but the *satguru* is the one who is always with(in) us. As

Guruji once told me, 'Where would you run away from God?'

One day Guruji forwarded me beautiful pictures of Athi Varadaraj, a Vishnu deity from Kanchipuram, which is the place of origin for the Sri Vaishnava lineage and its founder, Sri Ramanujacharya. I looked on the internet for more information and found that the deity was stored in an underground chamber inside the temple tank. He was brought out for worship for only 48 days after every 40 years, and it was exactly that period for His worship.

I thought to myself that this might be a unique chance to receive His blessing and asked Guruji if it was a good idea to travel there. What He answered was very touching and meaningful and served as a beautiful revelation to me:

'You see Him every day in the
people you are serving,
you just need to look beyond the external reality.'

Following His revelation to me, I would approach the people in the shelter home with the awareness that God resides in them and would occasionally perceive the Divine presence through their eyes or smile.

One day a man with throat cancer approached me crying. I reminded him of the ever-present

Bhagavan (God) within him and taught him the *mantra* '*om namo narayanaya*'. He looked at me with such depth that I felt as though I was being blessed by God himself. The magic of service started to unfold before me more and more.

When Guruji forwarded the pictures of the deity, He also sent the *Charama-shloka*, the key verse of the *Bhagavad Gita* (Chapter 18, Verse 66).

'Ignore all the religions and
SURRENDER TO ME without fears
and I shall forgive you from all your sins
and purify you.'

In His message, He included the following explanation:

'This is a simple verse said by Lord Krishna to Arjuna during the Kurukshetra war. Arjuna was loaded with lots of preaching given to him and finally summarising them, Krishna utters the above words. By surrendering oneself to Lord Krishna, a person is freed from all his sins. With faith and love, a person should surrender himself to the Lord.'

What Guruji sent me corresponded with my current life situation. I had received many blessings and a lot of teachings from Guruji, but I was still confused and not free of my mind. Through this message, I became aware that I could no longer hold onto the outcomes of my actions or try to become perfect. I just had to give everything to Him, good and bad, without holding anything back. To trust and to count on His grace was my aspiration.

As my three months in India were nearly over, the service at AIIMS was coming to an end. For me, this time had been an opportunity to experience that charity is an inner attitude and a quality. It can be done 'silently' without an organisation standing behind it.

I asked Guruji about it, and He wrote, 'It is to bring people to that awareness, that it is not just about giving money, but to participate.'

His words confirmed my experience in the shelter home: it was not primarily about financial support, but much more about open-hearted volunteers, teamwork and good organisation. The true help is in empowering people with education and spiritual awareness. Charity, in general, needs people who dedicate their time, or even better, their lives to it.

I kept Guruji informed about all the happenings in Delhi, and He seemed to be very pleased with it. He even suggested extending the period I could serve there. Eventually, we agreed that I would come back to Germany and, after some months, I could return to India for a longer period of time.

# Back in Germany

I came back to Shree Peetha Nilaya shortly before Navaratri and was eagerly waiting to see Guruji again after such a long period. He was standing outside the *ashram* with some devotees when we met. While touching His feet, He said, 'First time that I can say that I am really proud of you. You did a very good job there!'

It was an honour hearing those words from the *guru*, but His remark of 'first time that I can say', could not be ignored and kept me on the ground.

'Was it difficult for you to see the children dying?' Guruji asked.

I explained that the children had gone through a lot of suffering, and that in India the perception of life and death seemed to be different, more intertwined and natural. Moreover, by His grace, I was aware that the journey of the soul continues and that the physical death was not the end.

'Yes, it's a part of life', Guruji confirmed. 'The most important was to imprint the Divine Name in them.' He inquired further, 'What did you observe there?'

My answer came spontaneously, 'I realised that our part is to support them with spirituality.'

To which He commented, 'But the material is also important for them.'

He teased me by calling me 'Mother Theresa' and told me to return there for a longer period of time, during which I could continue with the charity projects and also get more people involved with them. He informed some of the *swamis* and those present to support me in this endeavour.

Later, when I was alone with Guruji, we talked about the situation in the world. I asked Him if initiating spiritual education in public schools would contribute to a bigger change.

'Such educational programs already exist', He replied.

'What, then, would help?' I enquired.

'To get enlightened; this would help.' He continued, 'If one gets enlightened, he brings the light to the world. In ancient times, when someone would leave the world in search for God, the villagers would support that person with food, etc. They knew that if this individual gets enlightened, everyone in the whole area would benefit.'

It was a good reminder, as He had emphasised several times, how important our own spiritual growth was. When the Self shines the light of God from inside-out, it reflects upon all of nature and through it, everything around transforms.

Before He walked away, I told Him that I had missed Him.

'I wish I could tell you the same', He replied. 'But I don't miss anyone, you all are inside of Me.'

I was glad to be back home. The last sunny days of the colourful fall season were fresh, and I could freely breathe again. After the pollution and masses of people in India, Germany appeared like an isolated and orderly place.

Meanwhile, as the *ashram* had to save on costs and space, there were many more *matajis* now living in the convent. We still had our beautiful church, and I was glad to resume with the prayers, enjoying the company of the saints. Since I was working on a book project and didn't have an office, I set up a small working corner in the church.

In my free time, I would meet with some of the residents for a walk, a chat or a cup of Turkish coffee, enjoying their company and trying to re-connect more with the whole community.

During the following days it was Navaratri, the biggest festival dedicated to the Divine Mother. We celebrated it in a richly and beautifully decorated tent for nine days. In the evenings, a large program with hundreds of guests was held which included prayers, *yagna*, *puja*, *abhishekam*, singing and dancing.

For most of the festival, I sat with the musicians, supporting the drumming, and feeling grateful to participate in such an uplifting spiritual event.

On the day of Katyayani Devi, Guruji gave a blessing to all the people in the form of the Divine Mother.

The conches were blown, and the bells rang as the curtain opened and we beheld Guruji in His majestic beauty as Devi. He was sitting on His *asana* with a mantle around Him, the *trishula* in His right hand and a crown on His head, giving Darshan.

When the *puja* for Him started, I was still drumming and had an excellent view from very close. The *mantras* were chanted, flowers and food were offered to Guruji, and the *arati* lamps were lit.

As I was looking at Guruji on His seat, His form suddenly started to transform. Instead of Him, the Divine Mother Herself in Her heavenly garments and divine beauty, with a goldish, porcelain-like face, was gracefully sitting on the *asana*, moving Her head ever so slightly. It was a glorious scene!

I put the djembe aside and fixed my eyes on Her to see if the vision would remain. Her appearance was smoothly changing and transforming into male forms, which I tried to identify. In relation to the main features which the forms had, I recognised Rama, Krishna, Shiva, Shirdi Sai Baba, Vamana, Buddha, Hanuman, Narasimha and, at the end, the Divine Mother once more, before She merged back into the appearance of Guruji. It was not a short vision as the forms were visible for some time.

The experience was unexpected, and I only shared it with a few people. After all, it was something personal; a reminder and an insight into who Guruji is and who resides in Him. Another time, when I called Him in a dream, a *Sudarshana* Chakra came as a mass of light, and behind it, an image of Narasimha appeared.

I still don't fully comprehend who Guruji is, but the experience showed that He is one with the Highest. More importantly, I understood the significance of having Him in this physical form with us, to be able to relate to Him, to establish a relationship with the Divine and grow in devotion. Guruji mentioned that He had only 127 incarnations on Earth, all with a specific role and mission.

At the end of November, we celebrated Babaji Day in the temple. I was drumming again and had a very good view of Guruji from the side. He was sitting close to the door, unnoticed by many people, when He closed his eyes and was immersed within Himself for a while. It came to my mind that He might be in communion with Babaji. Their connection is a mystery, as He often mentioned that between them there is no difference. On several occasions Guruji even appeared as Babaji.

Later in the evening, when Guruji gave a public talk, He announced that Babaji wanted Him to give the third level of Atma Kriya Yoga initiation. This was incredible news! Guruji started initiating into the first level of Kriya in 2007, into the second level in 2011, and now He would give the third level, individually, for the first time in 2019. We (the devotees) had eagerly been waiting for this moment. One needs to be ready to receive it, as each initiation or Shaktipat is amazingly strong and transformative.

He first asked how many of us had received the second Kriya initiation. Then He asked how many were practising it. His next question to us was how many were practising it daily. With each question the number of raised hands decreased and was finally reduced to only a handful.

At the end, Guruji said that all those who were practising the second level for the last five years without having missed more than five times, or one time a year, could come for the third level initiation.

Fortunately, I fell into this category. Guruji had initiated me into the second level in 2011, and since then, I have practised daily. I also remembered the dream from Albania, that the 'inner troubles' would disappear with the third initiation.

This was another unexpected grace received by Guruji.

After the Christmas and New Year's celebrations, I felt that the time had come to return to India and continue the charity work.

# Humanitarian Work in Delhi

I arrived in Delhi at the beginning of January and was surprised by the change of the weather as it was extremely cold. On the main street that led to AIIMS there were many tents set up for the patients during the wintertime. It was unthinkable how entire families, including small children, could endure living in such cold, harsh circumstances. The focus of the volunteers during this time was to provide warm clothes and blankets to the patients.

When I came back to the shelter home, the atmosphere was different. People were freezing and covering themselves with thick blankets. It was also obvious that there weren't very many children around. I found out that most of them were at the school and took this as a good sign that they had established the habit of going to school.

I went to the school to meet them, and when they saw me, they all ran towards me. After all, they were my little *bachche* (children). They did not know about my return and so it was a surprise for them. Without saying much, we hugged each other and shared some sweet moments.

In the following days, I resumed our program in the shelter home. One of the additional activities was head lice treatment. Every second Sunday the children, along with some adults, were treated with a special mixture to eliminate this unpleasant problem. Another volunteer also started creative work with the children making beautiful flowers out of coloured paper. The children were extremely talented with this activity.

On the main road of AIIMS, I encountered several other children staying on the street with their sick parents. I brought those who were staying for a long time to the school where they received good care from the teachers. Among them were two sweet sisters who, with their sick mother and two-month-old brother, were living in a tent while their alcoholic father tried to earn some money. The children looked like angels, but the elder girl started begging on the street in the market despite her mother's disapproval. The teachers at the school stepped in and gave her the necessary support to stop begging.

Help was needed everywhere but my call was to bring some essential change regarding basic needs.

On one occasion I had the opportunity to meet with the director of the AIIMS shelter home. He was in charge of many more shelter homes in Delhi. The main topic we discussed was the hygiene of the home and the people staying there.

During my previous stay in Delhi, together with the other volunteers, we organised a cleaning day at the AIIMS shelter that involved both volunteers and the residents themselves. All of the mattresses and belongings were removed and the whole space was cleaned. Everyone enjoyed the good teamwork, and we had a lot of fun with the kids. After engaging in this cleaning day, everyone was left feeling blessed.

Shortly after cleaning up, the shelter received new mattresses and bed sheets. Unfortunately, the hygiene had not been maintained; the bedsheets were not washed, and the general cleaning did not continue. There were additional obstacles in maintaining proper hygiene such as non-functional bathrooms, a lack of space and overall poor organisation.

The director was very open to cooperate and make improvements, and we agreed to start a hygiene project in the AIIMS shelter home, eventually expanding to many more. The project involved the purchase of an industrial washing machine, training of the caretakers on proper hygiene and cleanliness, identifying and removing any obstacles in each particular home, and implementing a new system for hygiene.

I started having regular meetings with the director and the first steps towards cleanliness were already visible.

I also met with another organisation who took care of sex-workers (the women who work as prostitutes) and their children in Delhi. It was moving to hear the stories of how the women ended up in this line of work. Most of them had been sold or kidnapped and forced into it. Some even grew up in brothels as prostitutes. It was unbelievable what these women went through. What amazed me most was that they were still able to live life just as all other people do, smiling, making jokes, and with a family and children of their own.

One area that the organisation helped with was the general care and education of the women and their children. Those who were ready and willing, were supported in the difficult process of leaving their profession and starting a new life. The volunteers were young and motivated with a spiritual approach, which I appreciated.

My role was to visit and teach the women who had already left, or were about to leave, their life of prostitution. We met weekly for *yoga* and breathing exercises, meditation, *satsang* and OM Chanting.

The best part, however, was still to happen: we all awaited Guruji's visit to the shelter home and His Darshan in Delhi. The children already knew about Guruji. They had seen His pictures, heard stories about Him, watched videos and listened to His songs. In preparation for His visit, the children started making paper flowers and other decorations, and we practised a song, partly in English, which they would perform in front of Him.

When this special day finally came, nearly all of the AIIMS volunteers, the director and a volunteer from the sex-worker organisation, gathered to meet Guruji. The children were given the best clothes to wear and each one had their hair made up nicely. One of the volunteers, who became Guruji's devotee, organised the clothes and a hairdresser. The shelter was decorated with colourful paper garlands made by the children, while Bhakti Marga music played in the background.

When Guruji arrived with a large group of His devotees, we all rushed to greet Him. People stood up to see Him and the children surrounded Him. They had made a beautiful paper garland for Him, which was hung around His neck by a blind boy, who greeted Guruji with the words, 'Open the eyes of my heart Lord, I want to see You.'

Upon entering the shelter home, Guruji filled the whole space with His presence. He walked through the entire place greeting and talking to the residents. He also addressed the volunteers, encouraging us to continue with the service. Additionally, He blessed the children and gave them sanctified rice. A few of the children wholeheartedly embraced Him, while others touched His feet or bowed down. People received Him with great respect.

After the children sang a song, Guruji gave a gift to everyone. In return, every child gave Him a handmade flower. We ended our program in the shelter home and moved on with the volunteers to a private place for a gathering and dinner with Guruji.

The next day Guruji was going to give Darshan in Delhi. The plan was to go with the children and their families in two buses to receive His blessing. Another volunteer and I arrived a bit early to the shelter home in order to make sure that everyone was ready in time.

Again, the residents were dressed in their best clothes. The women wore colourful saris with their beautiful, long, black hair bound together and a little bit of makeup, while the children wore shiny traditional clothing with nicely decorated hair.

We joyfully walked together to the main road towards the buses. The first bus was full but the second one was only half-full. While the other volunteer counted the people, I went back to see if any more residents wanted to join us.

When I returned to the bus with a few more people, the volunteer informed me that both buses were already full. I wondered about this since the second bus had been half-full only a short time ago. As I went inside, I saw many new faces and some unknown families. I asked them who they were, and they told me that they were patients from the neighbouring tents who had overheard about the event and wanted to join us. I thought to myself that this could only happen in India, and with a smile, agreed to it. God has His own ways of calling people. Finally, with 138 people loaded into two buses, we cheerfully made our way towards the Darshan venue.

Given that the behaviour of the people from the shelter home could be wild at times, I asked them during the drive to behave nicely at the Darshan. I role-played a few examples, saying in broken Hindi, 'Not like this', and then made some polite gestures saying, 'Like this.' They all laughed and indicated that they understood.

As we got out of the bus, they all stood nicely in a long line and moved towards the Darshan place. My heart melted, observing them. Having become part of my family, they were now joining my bigger Bhakti Marga family. In humility, they entered the Darshan hall and filled all the free space.

The venue was in a nice area of Delhi, in a huge, noble hall like an opera house. The musicians and Guruji's chair were already on the stage. When the *bhajans* began, we all clapped along and some of the children danced. One child was blind, another was deaf and mute, and the next one could not stand on his feet, but they all participated joyfully.

When Guruji arrived, the excitement reached its peak. A girl suffering from cancer and who was counting her last months of life, offered Him petals during the *Guru-stotram*. Guruji then gave a speech mentioning, 'these beautiful children from AIIMS hospital', as an example of simplicity and acceptance.

When Darshan started, the people from the shelter home went first, since the plan was to depart as soon as the last person had received the blessing. I was helping manage the line of people and was deeply touched by Guruji's boundless love and service to humanity as I watched Him receive and bless one person after another. Everyone was equally important to Him. After the last person finished, we all went to the buses together and departed.

The next day, the residents shared how much they had enjoyed the event. A blind boy told his mother that when he received Guruji's blessing, he felt something very soothing in his heart. Some of the girls and women were overwhelmed with the experience. Others wanted to know more about Guruji.

It was cute that the small children, who knew about Waheguru (the almighty God) from some of our Sikh volunteers, thought that Guruji was

WaheguruJi Himself who had finally come to visit them. They asked if Guruji slept and ate and where His abode was. How sweet the children were and how innocently they could perceive the Truth. I was so proud of them!

It was at this time that the coronavirus started spreading around the world. Since I had my own opinion about it, it didn't bother me at first. I continued visiting the shelter home, to cense the space and sing the Name of God with the people. My *seva*, however, was drastically affected when the lockdown came. All transportation was cut off and no one could move about the city without first getting permission from the police. The situation quickly became more and more serious.

One morning, I woke up very early and heard the words, 'Nature will punish you in the worst way for participating.' I then saw a vision of our planet completely covered with a whitish, stifling atmosphere. I didn't understand the meaning of it but was deeply concerned. Was it because I hadn't taken the situation seriously enough and had continued going to the shelter home? Many people at the home were sick with a weak immunity, and I couldn't behave irresponsibly towards them.

I decided to send Guruji a message about it. He was still in Vrindavan and already online at five in the morning. He replied right away, advising me to stay at home for the following days and to focus on my *sadhana* practice. Seeing His message, I felt calm again and was deeply grateful that He was always there for us, keeping everything under control even if the world seemed to go crazy.

It was not obvious what Guruji was doing for us, but at that moment I felt His sacrifice again, like a mother who is always there for her children, caring and holding them in her lap. I also asked Guruji if I could come to Vrindavan in case the situation gets worse, but He wrote that it was impossible due to the strict regulations. He ended the message with, 'Delhi must be calm and nice', which I took as a hint to enjoy this special time in the capital of India.

Relieved, I went back to bed to rest a little bit longer and had an interesting dream: I saw Guruji and wanted to run towards Him. He made a sign with His hand to remain where I was. I stopped, considering for a moment that I might have the virus and needed to keep my distance. At the end, Guruji made a gesture that He would come to me.

On another occasion, He came in my dream, giving me a book in my hand, to write 'theatre plays'.

In the following days, I did what Guruji had always wanted me to do: to search for the inner communion with Him, and to connect with Him from inside my heart.

Due to various reasons, I had always been resistant to taking this step in the past. When He was physically present, I wanted to connect with Him on that level. Moreover, when going into deeper concentration, I would feel a strong pressure in my chest and could not bear it for very long.

Now, however, seemed to be the right time for that step. As it is said, 'When you take one step towards God and *guru*, He takes a hundred towards you.'

During this period, Guruji did live *japa* and *satsang* for His devotees and followers daily. After performing *puja*, I would have lunch and finish all my tasks before starting my Atma Kriya Yoga practice. The third initiation I had received had opened the door for a deeper inner experience. After finishing with the practice, I would wait for *japa* to start. There was no pressure as everything in the outside world seemed to be on hold, and the present moment could take its place.

I would sit, relaxed on the ground, and my whole being would be still. With a Tulsi *mala*, the holy basil prayer beads, I would repeat the *mantra* simultaneously with Guruji, at the same time imagining Him inside of myself. While He is always with us, it is difficult for the mind to grasp where, what or how to connect to Him. But during this time, He was just there in the way which has been described: 'God is even closer to us than our own breath'. The load from my shoulders would drop off and I would be able to find rest within myself. Like Christ said, 'Come to Me, all who labour and are heavy laden, and I will give you rest.' The invisible layers around my chest would release and make space for the feeling of freedom. When Guruji would start with the ensuing *satsang*, I would end the meditation and feel fulfilled and satisfied from inside.

I even started to enjoy Delhi and would go for evening walks, admiring the beautiful variety of flowers and plants in the parks. There would often be a fragrant breeze in the air, and everything seemed to be in tune and a part of a bigger symphony. How simple and clear life appeared in those moments, and I asked myself how it was possible to so easily forget that fact. How silly it was to blind ourselves with material concerns and worries and to lose sight of the higher perspective of life. But this all seemed to be a part of His divine play and mystery.

I could have continued my life in this way, but two dear devotees started insisting on my return to Germany due to the unpredictable situation in India. Again, I asked Guruji about His opinion and He answered, 'Try to go back to Germany as soon as possible.'

My assumption had been that the situation would get worse and I called the German embassy for more information. The only option was to register for an evacuation flight, which they would maybe organise in the following weeks.

In the meantime, I continued with the daily walks along the empty streets of Delhi. On one of those evenings, I encountered a group of labourers who had lost their jobs and homes due to the lock down. They had found accommodation in a shelter home nearby and were waiting for the distribution of the food. I brought them some milk and chocolate, intending to visit them again on the following day. I also wrote to Guruji about it, as I saw that it was a chance to continue the service nearby. He insisted, however, on my immediate return to Germany.

As the importance of going back became clearer, I made additional efforts to find a flight. On the advice of the embassy, I found and booked an evacuation flight organised by the Netherlands. The flight was scheduled in a few days' time which meant I had to arrange everything very quickly.

When I wrote to Guruji about it, He expressed His interest to fly back as well, along with the team of *prabhus* who had followed Him to India. I immediately called the airline, but it was late and impossible to reach anyone. Looking on the website I could only see the flights for the following months, not for the following week. I tried again and again, but nothing was possible.

When I looked one last time, the same flight which I was on, was displayed. I immediately called a *swami* who was with Guruji and forwarded the link to him. In the next half hour, they all booked their flights! Just as soon as the flights were booked, the link disappeared again and some more people who wanted to leave India with Guruji were not able to do so.

During the next day, after talking to the German embassy several times, we all received the necessary permissions to travel to the airport and leave the country.

It was such a wonderful surprise to fly back home together with Guruji, and I remembered the dream where He had signalled to me that He would come to me.

On my last day in Delhi, I managed to visit the AIIMS shelter home to say goodbye to everyone as I didn't know if and when we would ever see one another again. Late that night I reached the airport and waited for the others to come. Guruji, along with His team arrived shortly after me, strictly following all the regulations for the coronavirus.

At that moment, I remembered how, a few years previously, Guruji had repeatedly said that if people do not change, nature will make them change. He also mentioned that something bigger was about to happen, but that He could not reveal it because our minds would make up their own story about it. During the daily *satsangs* in India, Guruji pointed out that this was the time and opportunity for people to change. In private circles He said that if humanity does not change now, it will have to learn in the future through suffering.

From a higher perspective, this situation seemed to be a necessary step in order to stop the crazy pace of the world. Humanity has become unaware of the fact that we are destroying our planet, eating and killing animals, exploiting the resources freely given by nature, and even abusing each other. We have forgotten that sooner or later *karma* will catch up and teach us the necessary lessons we must learn. As it is stated in the *Bhagavad Gita*, we all are part of nature and she reflects back the way we treat her.

At the airport, Guruji dropped hints that it would take a long time before the charity work in India would be able to resume. The evacuation flight was very unusual with a slight sentiment of being in a state of war, but with Guruji on board, it was a 'heavenly flight'.

## Coming Home

Upon our arrival back home, the spring weather in Germany was beautiful with fresh, breathable air. The fields around the *ashram*, which I missed while in India, were covered with new, light green and yellow growth, and thc trees were blooming and fragrant.

I would have preferred to go straight to the convent, but due to the required two-week quarantine because of the virus, that was impossible. However, being in the quiet *ashram*, closed off to the public, was a sublime experience. The residents took good care of us, bringing food and *prasad*, or anything else we needed, to our door. They also seemed to appreciate the peaceful period without the constant rush, which had been the routine previously at the *ashram*.

After the quarantine, I moved to the convent. Due to the current situation, there was only one sister staying there, taking care of the house, while all the others had temporarily moved to the *ashram*. I had missed our church and enjoyed having the company of the saints again. I also appreciated the daily temple prayers in the *ashram* much more than ever before. My increased gratitude was due to being back home with Guruji, having had all the experiences in India which made me stronger and more mature. I was so grateful for His mercy and endurance with us. I felt Guruji's enormous Love for creating Bhakti Marga, the *ashrams* and the *sanghas*, as our shelter place, keeping us on the spiritual path and guiding us towards God's Lotus Feet.

After my arrival in Germany, I had a pleasant dream where I was resting my head on Guruji's leg, feeling safe and cared for. At the same time, a big crack on our planet was visible, which was separating the earth.

In the following days, I started to become aware of the bigger picture of Guruji's incarnation on earth at this specific time. He came as a support for the whole of humanity and the world itself. As Krishna states in the *Bhagavad Gita* (Chapter 4, Verses 7-8):

'Whenever there is a decline in *dharma* (righteousness), and an increase of *adharma* (unrighteousness), it is then that I manifest Myself. For the protection of the good, for the destruction of the wicked, and to establish *dharma*, I incarnate Myself from age to age.'

I continued to practise Atma Kriya Yoga and with each day, my inner connection with God and *guru* became stronger. A similar state to the one which I experienced after the *brahmacharya* initiation started to awaken. I was calm and felt undisturbed by the outside, or at least I could choose not to be disturbed. I understood that everything happens for a reason and is a preparation for the next step in life. All of the people who come into our life, including those who hurt us, are in some way contributing to our progress. We just need to accept and to trust in what life is offering to us. By acceptance of what is, our *dharma* can unfold.

I remembered the dream I had in India where Guruji requested me to write the theatre plays and so I started writing about my personal experiences with Him. After all, life is a big theatrical play and we are the actors. Depending on how we view ourselves we become the actors in an adventure, a comedy or a drama. The stage director is God Himself, who hands out the roles according to our abilities and merits. The moment we realise that it is all only a play, we can relax and be ourselves.

One night, when I closed my eyes, I perceived something from the old times:

I was a young man with a *shikha* staying in an *ashram* with a *guru* who was very affectionate towards me. He disclosed to me that I was already self-realised and that this was my last life, after which, I would be God-realised and would not have to incarnate again in this world. I saw myself listening to Him and receiving His words with great delight.

Later in the vision, when passing by His cottage, I happened to hear Him saying something contradictory to some other disciples. I became upset thinking that my *guru* was a cheater and turned against Him, destroying and setting everything around me on fire. I saw myself repeatedly try to harm Him, while observing His serene, though sad expression, in response to my downfall. Once everything was on fire, I hid myself in a cave.

When the scene was over, I opened my eyes and felt peaceful. Perhaps the many years spent in the *ashram* had made me strong and detached enough not to judge myself anymore. Was my downfall from that life the reason for my occasional, uncontrolled breakdowns in this life and my emotional relationship with Guruji? The connection with the *satguru* is not only from this life but is a continuation from many lives before. Maybe all those experiences were needed to increase my longing for God so that one day I could return with a burning heart and gratitude.

I remember Guruji explaining the difference between self-realisation and God-realisation. It is the difference between knowing the soul, which can be reached by our own effort, and knowing God, which is only possible through His Grace. To perceive our True Self is not the final realisation and state of consciousness. A self-realised person is still bound by *karma* and can fall. Ultimately, that person would, however, reincarnate as a *bhakta*, a devotee, to develop a serving and loving relationship with God in His fullness. Guruji said that many people around Him have already gone through the process of self-realisation and many saints are incarnated as His devotees in order to experience the fullness of God.

Many years ago, during the eighteen days of the *Bhagavad Gita* lectures with Guruji, I had a dream with an insight of myself, being a certain part of a body. When the scene zoomed out, I perceived just a glimpse of a vibrant, luminous, and immeasurable human-shaped Form encompassing everything. This vision confirmed to me that, just like in the *Bible*, we are 'created in His image, in the image of God' and that He is not far away for, 'in Him we live and move and have our being', and 'we are indeed His offspring'.

* * * * *

My life journey continues by living in the *ashram* with the *satguru* and a spiritual community, learning and growing day by day. I don't know what tomorrow will bring, but I know that He is a Master, and His plan is a Master Plan, from the beginning of our existence until our blissful hearts rejoice in Him again! I know that in every moment and in each breath, He is there, waiting for us to awaken and return to Love!

How beautiful it would be to enjoy the Path of Devotion together, with the awareness that we are in Him and He is in us. How extraordinary is the incarnation of the Living Master, the incarnation of the Highest in the present time.

Let us celebrate His presence!

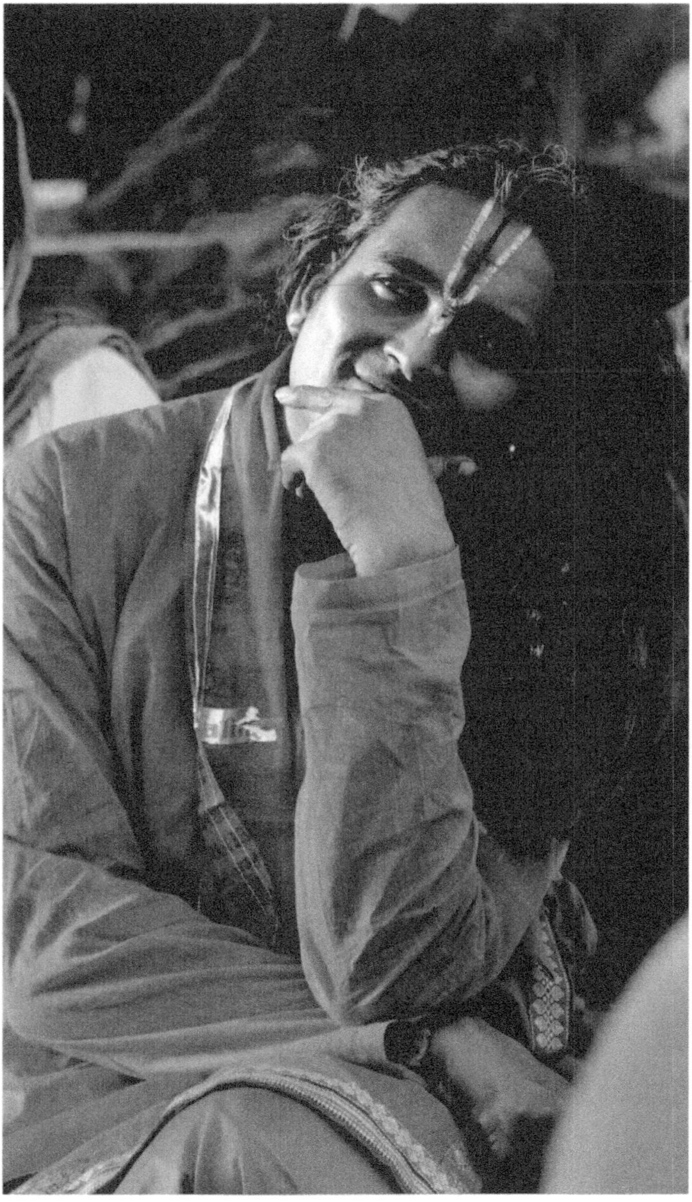

Paramahamsa Vishwananda

*Brahmacharya* Initiation in 2006

Balkan tour in 2006

Darshan in Romania in 2017

Darshan in Vrindavan in 2020

Guruji with the nuns

The 'Living Christ' icon

Travelling in Egypt

With children from the shelter home in Delhi

Guruji visiting the shelter home in Delhi

*Satsang* with Guruji at the *Ashram*

Paramahamsa Vishwananda during a Darshan

The Ashram 'Shree Peetha Nilaya' in Germany

The Ashram residents during a retreat with Guruji in Lanzarote

*Thank you for reading this book.*
*May the blessings of the Masters*
*be upon you!*

If you would like to know more about
Paramahamsa Vishwananda, Bhakti Marga or
Atma Kriya Yoga, please go to:
www.bhaktimarga.org

If you would like to know more about the charity
work, please go to: www.bm-charity.org

## Recommended reading:

**Just Love:** A Journey into the Heart of God
***Sri Guru Gita*:** Commentary on the Mysteries of the Guru-Disciple Relationship
***Bhagavad Gita* Essentials**
**Krishna & Christ, Vol 1** – Timeless Principles of the Hindu & Christian Faith
**Krishna & Christ, Vol 2** – Similarities and Inspirations of Their Lives

# Glossary

***Arati*** - a Hindu ceremony in which lights with wicks soaked in ghee are lit and offered to the Divine.

***Abhishekam*** – a Hindu ceremony of pouring water or other sacred substances on a deity while chanting *mantras*.

**AIIMS** – All India Institute of Medical Sciences

***Amrita*** – Divine Nectar

**Akathist** – a hymn dedicated to a saint, holy event, or one of the persons of the Holy Trinity.

***Asana*** – a seat or sitting pad

***Atma*** - individual soul or essence.

**Atma Kriya Yoga** – ancient *yoga* system revived in modern times by Paramahamsa Vishwananda and Mahavatar Babaji, https://bhaktimarga.org/yoga-meditation/.

***Avatar*** – 'Divine Descent'; descent of a deity/God on Earth, who comes to elevate and liberate those who have attained to the state of self-realisation, to destroy evil and end persecution and calamity on Earth, thereby restoring *dharma.*

**Babaji** - Paramahamsa Vishwananda's *satguru* and the *paramguru* of Bhakti Marga, who agreed to remain in a physical body to protect and oversee the long-term spiritual evolution of mankind and our planet. His Grace flows through Atma Kriya Yoga and all that Bhakti Marga offers.

***Bhagavad Gita*** – 'Song of the Lord', one of the most important and the best known religious texts of Hinduism, part of the great Indian epic *Mahabharata.* It is a dialogue between the warrior-prince Arjuna and the Lord, Sri Krishna at the Battle of Kurukshetra, describing the main concepts of the Hindu Scriptures; the belief in one God and the underlying unity of all existence. The text instructs how one must elevate the mind and soul to look beyond appearances and reach the ultimate goal of life. *Bhakti* (devotion) is introduced as the easiest means in achieving this.

***Bhajans*** – 'singing to glorify God', devotional songs and hymns.

***Bhakta*** - devotee or individual who practises *bhakti* or *Bhakti Yoga.*

***Bhakti*** – devotional worship directed to the Divine.

**Bishma** – one of the central pillars in the ancient Indian epic *Mahabharata*, who influenced the turn of events in the epic by his various acts.

***Charama-shloka*** – final and definitive message delivered in *Bhagavad* Gita by Sri Krishna.

**Darshan** - 'divine sight', looking upon or being in the presence of a temple deity, a master, or Divinity. A moment of seeing and being seen by the Divine.

***Dharma*** – the cosmic order or law, including the natural and moral principles that apply to all beings and things. Dutiful observance of this law in one's life; right conduct.

***Gayatri-mantra*** - highly revered mantra from the *Rig Veda*, which declares appreciation to the Divine.

***Giridhari*** – 1. another Name for Sri Krishna; The Lifter of Govardhan Hill.
2. Paramahamsa Vishwananda's *murti*, which once belonged to Mirabai, a prominent Indian Vaishnava Saint.

**God-realised** – self-realised beings who by grace of God or *satguru* receive the divine vision and are freed from the cycle of birth and death.

***Guru-stotram*** – a 14-verse praise to the *guru* from a sacred text known as the *Guru Gita* (part of a larger scripture called the *Skanda Purana*).

***Honout*** – anointment in the Coptic Church, mixture of powder made of different spices.

**Hanuman** - the faithful servant of Rama, the symbol of strength and devotion, whose exploits are described in the Ramayana.

***Hanuman-chalisa*** – the praises of Lord Hanuman, composed by Goswami Tulsidas.

***Hiranyagarbha-lingam*** – 'universal womb' or 'golden egg', the source of the creation of universe or the manifested cosmos in Vedic philosophy.

**Holi** – the Hindu spring festival in honour of Krishna, also known as the 'Festival of Love' or 'Festival of Colours'.

***Ishtadeva*** – worshipper's closest personal Divinity, favourite deity (from all lives).

***Japa*** – the repetition of the Divine Names

***Jiva*** – an embodied soul

**Just Love Festival** – annual spiritual and musical festival of Bhakti Marga.

***Karma*** – the law of action and reaction; the consequences of one's actions which need to be experienced in due time, binding the Self to the material nature and rebirth.

**Katyayani Devi** –the sixth form amongst Nava-Durga, or the nine forms of Divine Mother Durga, worshipped during the Navratri celebrations.

***Kirtan*** – the call-and-response chanting/singing of hymns and *mantras* performed in India's *bhakti* devotional traditions.

**Krishna** – the eighth *avatar* of Maha-Vishnu/Narayana. A manifestation of the Supreme Being, described in Hindu scriptures, such as the *Bhagavad* Gita, *Bhagavata Purana* and the *Brahma-samhita*.

**Krishna Janmashtami** – the appearance day of Krishna.

***Kumkum*** – red turmeric powder (used in Bhakti Marga to make the *tilak*/mark on the forehead).

***Kund*** – container in which the *yagna* fire is put in and all the offerings are made.

***Lingam*** – representation of Lord Shiva as pure consciousness, awareness, and infinity in an egg-like form.

***Maha-abhishekam*** – 'great' *abhishekam* performed on bigger murtis.
See '*abhishekam*'

**Maha-Lakshmi** – Divine Mother, consort of Maha-Vishnu/Narayana, and Goddess of wealth, fortune, power, beauty, and prosperity.

***Maha-prasad*** – remnants of the food offered to and eaten by the Divine or a *guru*.

**Maha-Vishnu** (Narayana or Hari) – the Supreme Being within Vaishnavism, described as having the divine blue colour of water-filled clouds, with four arms, holding a *Padma* (lotus flower), *Kaumodaki* (mace), *Panchajanya* (conch) and a *Sudarshana-chakra* (discus weapon). See also 'Narayana'.

**Mahavatar Babaji** – see '*Babaji*'

***Mantra*** - Vedic sacred word or phrase repeated as a prayer or during meditation, which creates a powerful vibration, focusing and transforming the mind and uplifting the soul.

***Mataji*** – 'mother', addressing a female devotee in Bhakti Marga.

***Mudra*** – 'gesture' or pose to stimulate different parts of the body and to affect the flow of energy.

***Murti*** – a consecrated statue, containing the Divine.

**Narasimha** – the fourth *avatar* of Maha-Vishnu/Narayana, who incarnated in a fierce form as part-lion and part-man to destroy evil.

**Narayana** – 'resting place for all living entities', Supreme Being (including his different *avatars*) in his infinite, all-pervading and transcendental form. In the *Bhagavad* Gita his 'Vishwarupa' (Universal form) is described as being beyond the ordinary limits of human perception or imagination.

**Navaratri** – annual Hindu festival celebrated in the spring and in the autumn over nine nights in honour of Divine Mother (Nava-Durga), where each day one of Her different aspects/manifestations is worshipped.

**OM Chanting** – Healing method given to the world by Paramahamsa Vishwananda and Mahavatar Babaji, as a part of Atma Kriya Yoga (https://bhaktimarga.org/yoga-meditation/).

***Padukas*** – *guru's* footwear/sandals worshipped by their devotees.

**Panduranga** – 'white coloured God', another name for Krishna.

**Paramahansa Yogananda** - an Indian yogi and *guru* who introduced the teachings of meditation and *Kriya Yoga* in America and the West.

***Prabhu*** – 'master', addressing a male devotee in Bhakti Marga.

***Prakriti*** – the Creation, primal matter, or substance from which the universe evolves under the influence of the Supreme Being. In the *Bhagavad Gita*, *prakriti* is distinguished into *apara-prakriti*, material nature (5 elements, mind, intellect, and ego) and *para-prakriti*, spiritual nature (jivas, the embodied souls).

***Prasad*** – food offered to the Divine.

***Prema*** – pure, unconditional love that leads to highest devotion and surrender.

***Puja*** - devotional worship and prayers to the Divine.

***Purusha*** – Cosmic Being, the Self, consciousness, spirit.

***Pyaar*** – conditional love with affection; amour, amorous relationship.

**Radhe** - the main gopi (milkmaid), lover and companion of Sri Krishna during his youth. The embodiment of highest devotion and love for God.

**Rama** - the seventh *avatar* of Maha-Vishnu/Narayana, a manifestation of the Supreme Being and husband of Sita (described in the *Ramayana*).

***Rudraksha*** – dried seed from the Elaeocarpus Ganitrus tree, which relates to 'Lord Shiva's Teardrops', used for making a prayer rope.

***Samskaras*** - mental impressions, recollections, or imprints from the past, which manifest as tendencies, *karmic* impulses, or habitual potencies in life.

***Sangha*** – spiritual community or gathering of people.

***Sannyasin*** – renunciate of the world and of material desires

***Satguru*** – the 'true guru' who removes the darkness of ignorance and gives Divine Light to human beings, leading them throughout many lives to God-realisation.

***Satsang*** – a spiritual discourse

**Self-realised** – spiritual practitioners who by their own effort spiritually advance and get to know their soul.

***Seva*** - 'selfless service', acting selflessly and helping others in a variety of ways, without any reward or personal gain.

**Shaktipat** – Initiation into Atma Kriya Yoga; blessing and grace, given by Paramahamsa Vishwananda and Mahavatar Babaji to *kriya yogis*.

***Shikha*** – lock of hair, left on top or on the back of the shaven head of a male Hindu (monk). It signifies one-pointed focus on a spiritual goal, and devotion to God.

**Shirdi Sai Baba**- Indian spiritual Master and saint, manifestation of Dattatreya.

***Shiva-lingam*** – see '*lingam*'

**Shivaratri** – annual Hindu festival celebrated in honour of Lord Shiva (the third person of the

Trimurti, along with Brahma the Creator and Vishnu the Preserver).

***Srimad Bhagavatam*** – also known as the *Bhagavata Purana*, is *one of the* eighteen *Puranas*, highly revered by the devotees of Maha-Vishnu. It is a collection of stories about Narayana, His *avatars* and a detailed account of Sri Krishna.

**Sikh** - are people who adhere to Sikhism, a religion that originated in the late 15th century in the Punjab region of the Indian subcontinent, based on the revelation of Guru Nanak.

**Sri Yantra** – a sacred geometry of Divine Mother and the entire cosmos, used for meditation, protection from harmful influences and spiritual development.

***Sudarshana Chakra*** - most powerful discus weapon of Maha-Vishnu. See also 'Maha-Vishnu'

***Swami(ni)*** - 'Master of the Self'. A Bhakti Marga Swami/ni is tasked with carrying the presence of Paramahamsa Vishwananda and to spread His teachings and blessings.

**Theotokos** - Mother of God, used in the Eastern Orthodox Church as a title of the Virgin Mary.

***Tilak*** – a mark worn on the forehead as a religious symbol. Initiated devotees of Bhakti Marga wear the *tilak* on daily basis as a reminder to put God first in all doings.

***Trishula*** – a trident, a divine symbol, commonly used by Shiva and Devi (Divine Mother).

**Vaikuntha** - eternal heavenly abode of Narayana and Maha-Lakshimi. The highest state where the liberated souls abide, as eternal servants and lover of God.

**Vaishnava** – one who practises Vaishnavism

**Vaishnavism** – one of the major Hindu denominations devoted to the worship of Maha-Vishnu and His *avatars.*

***Vamana*** - the fifth *avatar* of Maha-Vishnu in the form of a dwarf Brahmin, who with three steps took back the three worlds from the *asuras* (demons) to give back to the *devas* (demi-gods).

***Vibhuti*** – sacred ash

***Vishnusahasranama*** - Sanskrit hymn which contains 1,000 names of Maha-Vishnu. It is connected to the epic *Mahabharata* and sung in honour of Sri Krishna.

**Waheguru** - term in Sikhism to refer to God, the Supreme Being or the creator of all.

***Yagna*** – Vedic fire ceremony where the participants chant *mantras* and make offerings to the Divine.

Printed in France by Amazon
Brétigny-sur-Orge, FR

31354857R00141